U.S. Customs

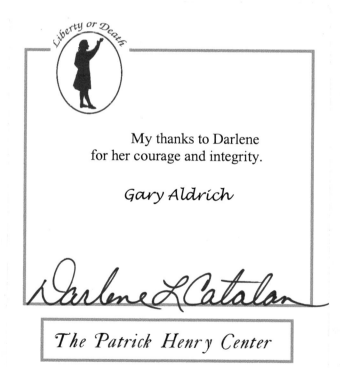

My thanks to Darlene
for her courage and integrity.

Gary Aldrich

Darlene L Catalan

The Patrick Henry Center

U.S. Customs

Badge of Dishonor

Darlene Fitzgerald-Catalan
Former Federal Agent

Authors Choice Press
San Jose New York Lincoln Shanghai

Authors Choice Press
an imprint of iUniverse, Inc.

For information address:
iUniverse, Inc.
5220 S. 16th St., Suite 200
Lincoln, NE 68512
www.iuniverse.com

Author photo courtesy of Ernie Bach and KISS Photo.

ISBN: 0-595-16795-0

Printed in the United States of America

Dedication

I dedicate this book to all the women and men in the Department of Treasury who have fought and are fighting the corrupt "good old boy" crony system and have suffered because they refused to be silent.

To my dad, Kelsie, a World War II veteran and survivor of the Battle of Guadalcanal, who taught me that the only thing worse than fear is regret.

To Ian Lawler, thank you so much for your undying support.

Contents

One Clear Voice
Foreword—by Gary Aldrich

For more than 26 years I served as a special agent with the Federal Bureau of Investigation. Part of my responsibility was to study and then attack the Mafia and other organized crime groups. All organized crime (OC) has similarities that enable criminals to avoid detection and capture. One useful tool is "Omerta"—the Mafia-inspired code of silence—the ordered secrecy, making it impossible for "outsiders" to learn of their criminal conspiracies, illegal activities and weaknesses.

The classic way to maintain Omerta is to warn each member of the group that terrible things will happen to them if they violate the group's secrecy rules. For example, it is routine inside the Mafia and other violent OC groups to torture and then kill suspected "rats" who disclose information to the wrong persons—such as law enforcement officers. Even if the "rat" makes the disclosure accidentally, or with the best of intentions, the punishment is the same—torture, then death.

Sometimes, the OC members are so angry they destroy the whistle-blower's entire family. Or to make a point with a suspected "leaker," they may threaten, kidnap or kill one of their children. This is how they enforce the silence that protects them all.

After the informant is very publicly punished, anybody else who might have been thinking of disclosing information to outsiders will think twice. Thus, the blanket of protective secrecy is maintained.

When I went to work for the FBI there was another kind of silence in place. It was called the "Secrets Act" or some such official sounding name. There was also a group ethic in play that is fairly common in law enforcement. I was told in the strongest terms that nothing I learned on the job could be disclosed, except to prosecutors, judges and juries. Only the facts that I gathered to convict criminals could be disclosed, and if we had any corruption or incompetence inside the agency, we were to handle our "dirty laundry" ourselves, not letting anyone else know about it.

That was the group ethic then, and I suspect it is the same now. These twisted ethics fostered a "them against us" mentality. Such foxhole mentality helps bond workers together but can be dangerous if serious corruption is discovered. If there is a pattern of cover-up, who decides what gets to be hidden and what needs to be revealed? In the final years of my career, I witnessed significant damage to national security and to the reputation of the FBI as my agency bent over backwards for political reasons to please a reckless president and his corrupt administration.

Historically, the FBI has forbidden the disclosure of information to immediate family members. Moreover, FBI agents could not disclose serious wrongdoing to their own attorneys unless they first sought and received permission from the FBI. If they violated this rule, they were subject to dismissal for insubordination.

Federal agents were never to speak to the media unless they had permission, and then such occasions were closely monitored by management. Even when FBI special agents were called to testify in front of congressional oversight committees they were not able to speak candidly—they were accompanied by agency attorneys, ever ready to lower the boom if the agent's remarks were not part of the "party line" desired by the "front office." Agents deemed to be overly talkative were considered "disloyal" to the agency and the director, and upper management was promptly notified about such lapses. When agents spoke to outsiders, it was a well-known fact that their career hung in the balance.

It was the kiss of death to an FBI agent's career if it was learned that they had independently complained to their own senator or representative about any FBI missteps or shortcomings. Even if perfectly legal and highly useful to the Legislative Branch's oversight responsibilities, such contacts were, and still are, deemed to be disloyal and highly suspicious to the rest of the FBI group—especially management.

Some of this secrecy may be a good thing because secrecy protects national security and also protects important cases under investigation. After all, nobody wants the "bad guys" to learn about the progress of an investigation or weaknesses in any particular case. This is especially true today when our nation is under attack by foreign terrorists. Everyone understands that a certain amount of information should remain confidential.

It is also a truism that management is better informed and thus, logically, should be the group to officially disclose agency matters. But, what if management is a big part of the problem? Can we not assume that they would be less candid when called into question?

There is a difference between protecting secrets that have a bearing on investigations or national security, and hiding information that may indicate deep incompetence or corruption.

Furthermore, human beings are naturally eager to hide their shortcomings because they know if their flaws are available for review by higher management their careers will not be enhanced. They know they are better off career-wise if they are able to cover-up missteps and stupidity.

Agency chiefs also know that they will be scolded and held responsible if agents under their control make mistakes or become corrupted. So, "keeping the lid on" is part of the "group-think" that eventually takes over any bureaucracy—no matter how honest and decent the group was when it was first organized.

Most citizens do not realize this. Most honest, decent applicants who decide to make federal law enforcement their lifelong career are totally unaware of this. It's ironic that federal law enforcement agencies spend millions of dollars each year to find honest applicants. They consider honesty and integrity as major requirements for successful completion of the applicant process, but once hired, they indoctrinate new recruits into the ethic of the group, which includes the code of silence—the "ethic" of Omerta, the concept of a cover-up.

In some cases, newly minted honest federal law enforcement officers do not even complete academy training before they are faced with their first dilemma: to report untoward, unethical activity. Whether it's the cover-up of a simple-minded instructor who "hits" on the attractive new female recruits, or the inappropriate activities of fellow officers during their off-duty time, or even something more serious—the conflict between becoming a whistleblower, or "going along to get along," a conflict that begins early in each federal agent's career and continues on until the day they resign or retire.

Most always, such corruptions or lapses are minor in nature and can be overlooked without serious impact to the quality of the group, or to the mission of the agency.

But, increasingly—and for reasons that go far beyond my ability to explain in a mere book foreword—serious corruptions and instances of incompetence, "good-old-boy" isms, blatant examples of "careerism," and other destructive group-think activities have become a serious factor in the careers of too many good, hardworking, decent, and yes—honest—federal law enforcement officers. And all too often, federal agents spend as much time watching their backs for attacks from stupid or jealous management as they do working on the mission of putting the bad guys out of business.

It has become the reflexive response of every single federal agency, especially federal law enforcement, to attack the messenger—to attack the whistleblower who dares to come forward to question the low quality of management or work performance. Even when they try to surface serious corruption, or protect national security that has been weakened either purposely or by accident, whistleblowers are treated as pariahs, not worthy to sit at the same lunch table with decent people.

The FBI has made some progress since I came forward in 1996. This is exhibited in the respectful treatment of honest ethical dissenters and in the manner in which their complaints are taken more seriously. A new FBI director was just appointed, and it is hoped that he will be able to address the FBI's many management shortcomings. We will watch, and we will hope. Still, I've never seen a whistleblower publicly saluted by an FBI director or any other director of a federal law enforcement agency.

How did it get this way? How can we fix it? Why don't we celebrate those who are trying to make things better? Why do we allow bureaucrats free reign to punish these beleaguered, honest and courageous public servants who come forward?

I don't have all the answers. All I know is that U.S. Customs Agent Darlene Catalan and her loyal associates in the federal law enforcement agency in which they served, ran up against tremendous incompetence, and quite possibly, major corruption in the management ranks of those who are supposed to protect our borders.

They tried to work within the system as they were trained and told to do. Then they went to their legal representatives, who amazingly betrayed them. Then they went public, just as I had done before. I survived being a whistleblower, and I even prospered—and so will Darlene and her brave friends, with our help.

It is every citizen's responsibility to support our "ethical dissenters," those honest citizens who step forward to shine a light on that which is so obviously wrong. Someday the federal government will be forced to abandon the ethics of the Mafia—as it pertains to the disclosures of honest federal employees who are simply trying to right a serious wrong.

Sadly, I believe that will only happen after the general population loses its twisted fascination with and affection for corrupt politicians, antiheroes, and the Mafia.

But until that happens, our ethical dissenters will find their strongest support among the decent, law-abiding members of our society who know the difference between the protection of national security and the maintenance of a system of silence. Such enforced silence is nothing more than shelter for the incompetent and the corrupt who gleefully feed at the public trough.

Thank you, former U.S. Customs Agent Darlene Catalan. Your country owes you a debt of gratitude for stepping forward. You protected your country in the military. You wore a gun and a badge and protected us along the borders. Your revelations continue to protect us all.

Foreword

When Darlene Catalan and I first met in 1989, we were both Special Agents with the U.S. Customs Service in Los Angeles, California. Back then, when we were both in our late 20's, we were idealistic federal agents eager to do our jobs, believing wholeheartedly in the U.S. Customs Service mission: to investigate and prosecute violators of Customs laws. To us and all other agents we worked with, the bad guys were the outsiders. And in the early years of our careers, that was indeed the case. Though we worked in different offices, we saw each other on occasional surveillances or training days and forged a fast friendship. Over the years, we both achieved a great deal of recognition for our strong abilities as investigators and learned what it took to go after the "big boys" in the world of drug smuggling and money laundering.

Beginning in December 1997, our world and our belief in the agency to which we had devoted our lives began to disintegrate in front of our eyes. How could Darlene and I have known or even imagined the events which would descend upon us when we chose to exercise our lawful rights to engage in an administrative process under the Equal Employment Opportunity Commission (EEOC)? How could we have known that from then on, and to this date, our lives would be intertwined in a series of events that would result in our battling corruption and criminal activity at the highest levels of U.S. Customs? We fought alongside several other courageous Customs employees who chose to exercise their integrity in defiance of the lies and deceit of Customs managers and their cronies. From that moment forward, none of our lives would ever be the same. We would be harassed, threatened, intimidated, investigated by Internal Affairs on false charges, surveilled electronically, surveilled by agents within our own agency and ultimately forced to resign from jobs we had once dearly loved just to keep our honor and integrity intact.

There are those who say we gave up the fight by resigning in September 1999, and as for the corrupt management officials we found ourselves battling against, they applauded their victory thinking that was the last they would ever hear of Darlene Catalan and Sandy Nunn. They were wrong. For Darlene and I are not, and never will be, quitters. It's not in our blood. Our fathers, both highly decorated military officers, ingrained perseverance in us from the day we were born. Darlene's father was a World War II veteran and a survivor of the Battle of Guadalcanal; mine was an Air force pilot. No, we didn't resign just to quit and give up the fight. We resigned to keep our integrity and to protest the scurrilous treatment to which we were being subjected on a daily basis by corrupt managers who were abusing their authority and openly violating federal laws.

It has been over a year and a half since we resigned from our positions with Customs, but giving up was never an option for us. We have committed ourselves to bringing the truth to the people of this country because it is the right thing to do. Darlene has taken the first step in doing so by writing this book and describing in personal detail the abuses we were subjected to and the jeopardy our lives were placed in when we uncovered corruption of unimaginable proportions in one of the most powerful federal law enforcement agencies in our nation—the U.S. Customs Service. Darlene's account of the events and the people involved is both accurate and bone-chilling to those of us who experienced it firsthand. I highly encourage each and every American to read this book and know that, though some of the names have been changed, the facts themselves are absolutely true. When you are finished reading this account describing what really goes on within U.S. Customs, ask yourselves this: "If they can do this to federal agents within their own agency and get away with it, what could they do to me?" Customs has the broadest search authority of any agency in the United States, and their abusive practices towards their employees are beginning to spill into the public sector as evidenced by recent legal problems stemming from illegal searches of people re-entering the U.S. from foreign destinations.

The fact remains that the U.S. Customs Service is clearly a federal agency that abuses its authority, both over its employees and over the public at large. It is an agency that has gone to enormous trouble to hide its problems to Congress and to you, the taxpayer. It is an agency rife with corrupt management officials and their cronies. Clearly, it is an agency in serious need of an intensive GAO investigation, major internal reform, the removal of hundreds of corrupt managers either through termination or jail terms, and strict oversight by Congress and the taxpayers of this country. This agency has become arrogant in its practices, and the time has come for it to stop. The taxpayers of this country and the remaining good, decent, honest employees within the agency deserve much more than what they are currently receiving.

Read this book! And take the time to read Cathy Harris', "Flying While Black: A Whistleblower's Story." Her book details how she, a Customs Inspector from Atlanta, Georgia, blew the whistle on illegal search practices by Customs officials towards minorities returning from foreign destinations. Also look for my account of this national issue in my upcoming book, "The Dark Side of Justice." All in all, you will begin to learn just how extensive this issue really is and how it affects your family and your business.

It is said that knowledge is power. This is truly the case. We were the true insiders who saw the gross reality of corruption firsthand. We want to educate those of you who will read these accounts, listen and take a hand in bringing integrity back to federal law enforcement before the corruption becomes so great that it deteriorates our system of government and federal law enforcement agencies forever.

SANDY G. NUNN

President/CEO, Mirsan Consulting Group

National Spokeswoman, Association of Customs Employees for Change

Former Special Agent, U.S. Customs Service 1989-1999

Acknowledgements

I would like to give special thanks to my family who stood by me through the enormous stress this battle created. I also want to thank my parents who taught me to face life with a spine, and I apologize for all the worry I caused them.

I would like to thank the brave women and men who stood shoulder to shoulder with me and fought bravely against corruption, cronyism, discrimination and the glass ceiling within the U.S. Customs Service. These individuals endured tremendous stress, stress so great that it is likened in severity to that created by war. To Ruben Sandoval, Sandy Nunn, Ervin Rios, Cynthia Gonyea, Renado Gianini, Ricardo Sandoval, John Carmon and Cathy Harris: I am proud of each one of you for growing a spine and taking your best shot at the Mafia-style management firmly in place within the U.S. Customs Service. I know that this courage cost all of you dearly.

To our attorneys, Gastone Beebe and Thomas Allison: thank you for believing in all of us and for putting up with our many phone calls and insistent behavior. Thank you for educating us as to our rights as federal employees and how the EEO "system" is really designed to work only on behalf of the Mafia-style management employed in the U.S. Customs Service.

Special thanks to Gary Aldrich, author of *Unlimited Access*, and his staff at The Patrick Henry Center. I commend you and your foundation for the courage and support that you provide to honest cops attempting to get positive change in their agencies. You, Gary, are a brave soldier and a credit to the spirit your foundation represents: "Give me liberty or give me death!"

To the brave attorneys at the Government Accountability Project, a special note of appreciation. Your efforts in assisting whistleblowers through proposing much needed legislation is a demonstration of honor.

Special thanks to Sandy Nunn, Gary Aldrich, Sara Barbour and Leah Heisig for assisting with the final editing of this book. Their literary skills made this book much more legible to the average "non-law enforcement" person. And to Ernie Bach of KISS Photo for his assistance in the creation of graphics for this book.

Introduction

This book is based on a true story as seen through the eyes of female federal agent Darlene Catalan. Catalan tells of how federal agents in the Department of Treasury's U.S. Customs Service fought a courageous battle against cronyism, fraud, discrimination and corruption. Most of the names in this story have been changed, names of cases and operations have been changed, some characters have been combined and the sequence of events has been altered. This was done in order to protect innocent agents who are still working for Customs, as well as confidential informants, sources and ongoing related criminal cases and the pending federal civil litigation against the Customs Service.

Chapter One

The Murder

On December 17, 1990, Jason Fielding and his daughter Megan were driving home from Megan's school play in Long Beach, California. Jason was an attorney and a well established and well respected private investigator. He had been working on an investigation for a special Congressional committee in Washington, D.C. for the past 180 days. Jason had come home for a much-needed Christmas break and to see his daughter in her first school play.

Jason was 44 years old, and as a well-decorated, seasoned investigator, he had been hand-picked for special assignments by the government. His most recent investigation involved allegations of corruption in the U.S. Customs Service. Jason and his wife Anita had been married for seven years and had a beautiful home in Long Beach. Anita, a computer programmer, missed her husband terribly when he was gone. However, she was particularly tolerant of this last assignment because she knew that soon her husband would be home for good.

Anita had decided to stay behind at the auditorium to help the teachers clean up after the play. The plan was for Jason to drive six-year-old Megan home, feed her, spend time with her and tuck her into bed. Then he and Anita could have some quality time alone. Jason was a good man who loved his family very dearly. Megan was the apple of his eye. There has never been a child more loved by a father than Megan, and Megan adored her daddy.

The drive home from the play was full of fun and magic. Jason was an amateur magician and would always perform tricks for his daughter who idolized him. After a quick trip through the drive-through window at Burger King, they headed home. Jason opened his mouth wide while Megan tried to throw French fries into her dad's mouth. Once she hit him in the eye, and they had a good laugh. It was a cool, crisp Long Beach December evening, and Jason could taste the seawater on his lips as they drew closer to the ocean. It felt good to be home.

As Jason pulled the car into their driveway, the night-sensored lights came on. Jason helped Megan with her seatbelt, and the two of them grabbed the bags of fast food and headed into the house. Jason's hands were full, so pushed the car door shut with his foot. He never saw the darkly dressed, masked man come from behind the bushes. Megan gasped, drawing her father's attention towards her. He thought that she had closed her hand in the car door. Just then, three muffled shots filled the air. Megan watched in shock as her daddy collapsed to the ground like a bag of sand, the life drifting from him. Jason looked up at her in sorrow as if his last thoughts were of how tragic it was that his baby daughter had to see this traumatic thing. As Megan cried, the perpetrator fled.

Chapter Two

EEO

On November 11, 1996, Renado Gianini and I were on surveillance on Mill Street in San Bernardino, California. I was running Operation Black Widow with the San Bernardino Police Department and Special Agents (SA) of the Union Pacific (UP) and Burlington Northern/Santa Fe (BNSF) Railroads. We had a confidential informant that had given us information concerning an organization of thugs that was hitting railroad boxcars as they entered into Redlands and San Bernardino. So far that year, they had made off with approximately $11 million of Customs' in-bond merchandise. This same ring was supposed to be involved in the manufacturing and distribution of methamphetamine (meth/speed). We also learned that right in the middle of all of this was a crooked border patrol officer. We had been surveilling a particular crook who had been seen meeting with the border patrol officer for several days now, putting together enough probable cause to hit two suspected stash houses.

I was parked in an abandoned warehouse on Norton Air Force Base looking through binoculars at the crook's house on Mill Street. Renado was sitting a couple of blocks over with several other officers from his department. As I sat there, it hit me that my very first case with Customs had been right down the street. That's how I met Renado. We ended up seizing $72 million in precursors and lab equipment for manufacturing meth on that caper. I remembered how different Renado looked then, all narced out. His hair was long and he sported an earring; he basically looked like a thug. This was his undercover look. Renado was a very muscular, white male with red hair and a mustache—about 45 years old and handsome in a rugged way. "Now he wears a suit and tie most of the time, and I can hardly get him in the field with me," I thought, laughing to myself. That case was one of the first of many large seizures that I would make with no recognition from management of my work. I remembered how hurt I was to find out that, unlike others in my office, I would receive no award or even a word of commendation regarding this case. That's when a lot of my troubles began. My laughter turned to a headache.

I was brought back to the present when a van departed the residence on Mills Street, and we surveilled it to a number of locations dropping off stolen merchandise. A few hours later, Renado had the state warrant in hand, and we began kicking doors. The first place we entered was the main residence of our primary subject. As Renado took him to the floor and handcuffed him, a second guy ran out the back door. Another Task Force Officer (TFO), Ray, and I chased after him. I saw that the subject was overweight and wasn't going to last long. I just paced him. I was in good running shape and didn't want to catch up with him too quickly; I thought it better to let him wear himself down first. After a few minutes he was so out of breath that he fell to the ground, and I pounced on him. I secured the cuffs and sat on him to catch my breath. I started laughing and said, "Well fat boy, you better go on a diet if you're gonna stay in this line of work. You made this too easy for me." The search at this location yielded about $500,000 of stolen merchandise including TV's, designer clothes, VCR's and exercise equipment, all taken from the railroad.

We proceeded to the second location. We entered this "ghetto dive" apartment complex and walked through a tiny walkway between two walls. At the end there was a cast-iron gate. As we approached, a large black kid, about 15 years old, wearing an old army field jacket, opened the gate and walked towards us. The TFO I was with said to him, "Hey partner, would you hold the gate open for us, please?" The kid saw our raid gear and badges, gave us a dirty look and slammed the gate behind him, prohibiting our entrance. I had seen this look a hundred times before, that "I hate you" look of pure resentment and hopelessness. As he slammed the gate shut, the TFO and I both noticed what appeared to be the end of a rifle sticking out of his jacket sleeve. The TFO yelled, "Gun!" and we both grabbed him and shoved him against the wall.

Renado ran up to us and grabbed the guy, too. The TFO and Renado pinned his shoulders against the wall while I grabbed the object in his jacket and pulled out a riflescope. My immediate thought was that where there is a scope, there is a gun. Just then, the kid tried to jerk away and attempted to reach under his jacket. We were in a little alleyway with no more than four feet between each wall; it was a tight situation. As Renado and the TFO tried to push his shoulders back against the wall and control his arms, I tried to beat him to the gun. Grabbing his jacket, I pulled the bottom of it up and felt inside his belt area. Sure enough, there was a pistol sticking halfway out the front of his pants. As Renado grabbed the guy's arm and tried to wrench it behind him in an effort to stand him up straight so that I could grab the weapon, he lunged forward and bent over, trapping my hand on the gun in his belt. I could feel my bones being crushed. The suspect really started fighting us, trying to reach for the gun. He looked at me with such intensity that I felt he was determined to get the gun and blow my head off.

I knew that I had to get the weapon before he broke my hand and got it himself. I pressed my feet against the adjacent wall and pushed my shoulder into his chest in an effort to straighten his torso. As I was pushing against him with all my might, my heart was racing and my chest pounding. I pressed my shoulder and head into him and felt the energy drain from my body. As a mental defense mechanism, my mind started wandering to block out the pain. I saw flashes of green grass waving in the wind, and I could hear my kids laughing. Just then Renado screamed, "Get the gun, Dar! Get the gun!" A sudden rush of adrenaline pounded through my body, and I gave one last powerful push against the wall, pulling the gun out. It went flying, and I jumped to secure it. We wrestled the guy to his knees and cuffed him. Catching our breath, I looked at Renado. He was staring at me like the cat that caught the canary. "What?" I asked. "You just had to get your hands down a man's pants today somehow, didn't you?" I got up and pushed Renado off balance, and he fell over laughing. Renado knew that only he and Ruben (my Customs partner) could ever get away with that kind of joking with me. They were like brothers to me.

As we finished processing the evidence and booking the crooks, Renado said, "So, you and Ruben are really going to do this tomorrow, huh?" I looked at him uncertainly and said, "Looks like it." "Well Dar, for what it's worth, I think you guys are doing the right thing. It takes a lot of guts to do what you guys are doing. I know that in most agencies those complaints aren't received that well, to say the least." He shook my hand, and I smiled.

That night I could hardly sleep. I was still excited about having fought a 15-year-old gang banger for a gun, and worried about what Ruben and I were about to do the next day.

Morning came and my partner, SA Ruben Sandoval, and I went to the World Trade Center in Long Beach to meet with the equal employment opportunity (EEO) counselor on Ruben's EEO complaint. I was Ruben's key witness to the discrimination dealt him for several years at the hands of our group supervisor, Ivan Winkowsky. As bad as I thought Winkowsky had treated me for being a woman, it wasn't half as bad as his obvious discrimination against Ruben for being a Latino. Ruben and I had been partners and office mates for about six years. Prior to Customs, Ruben spent seven years with Secret Service and seven years with the Fontana Police Department as a dog handler. Ruben was 41 years old, about 5 feet, 10 inches tall, and a well-built, handsome Latino male. He was an excellent agent with a street savvy confidence and ESP about him that kept us out of trouble on more than one occasion. I remember how nervous and out of character Ruben was about meeting with this EEO counselor. It was as if his streetwise ESP was kicking in, and we were both choosing to ignore it for the first time, a mistake we would later regret.

The EEO counselor was a young black agent named Victor Ross. Ruben and I told him about all of the unfairness that had been going on at the RAIC/Riverside (Resident Agent in Charge) office for several years. I was surprised that he so firmly suggested we contact an attorney. I did not think much about this at the time, but if I had known then what I know now, I would have listened more closely to his advice and hired an attorney much sooner. Now I know that these words were not just simple advice, but a subtle warning.

Mr. Ross also recommended that we consider filing a class action EEO complaint and talk to another EEO counselor, Ms. Mary Conales. Her office was just down the hall, so after our interview we stopped by her office. Ms. Conales was a very beautiful, longhaired, Latino woman in her late twenties. Upon first meeting her, she came across as a bit sneaky and coy. Her mannerisms and gestures reminded me of a Latino version of Scarlet O'Hara in *Gone With the Wind*, a slippery little vixen. We told Conales that we were interested in filing a class EEO complaint. We explained to her what had been going on at the RAIC/Riverside, the small field office where we worked, and that Ruben had already filed an individual EEO complaint. I told her that I, too, intended to file a complaint, but would consider filing a class action if it was more appropriate. She played ignorant, acting like she did not know much about the class complaint system. Red flags went up in my mind and I questioned her integrity. Why, as a supervisor, did she not know anything about class EEO complaints? She told us that she would look into it and get back to us.

Chapter Three

The Threats Begin

On November 30, 1996, SAIC/LA (Special Agent in Charge) Drake Brinkley spoke at a congratulatory pizza party for all those who had recently been promoted. Drake Brinkley was the agent in charge of the large Office of Investigations for all of Los Angeles, as well as several RAICs in southern California and Nevada. Brinkley was a white male, approximately 49 years old and appeared rather unassuming. The congratulatory speech he gave pertained to the recent promotion in which Ruben and I had been passed over, while agents with much less experience, less time with Customs, and much less significant casework were promoted. All of these agents also happened to be white males, a trend I would learn was typical for promotions in Customs. Brinkley arrogantly announced to all attendees, "Someone at the RAIC/Riverside has filed a grievance, and now I have to deal with them." I had the wisdom not to attend this party, but was told of Brinkley's subtle threat. I wondered, though, how Brinkley knew so quickly that we had filed a complaint. Ruben's complaint was still at the informal and anonymous stage and was, by EEO policies, supposed to be confidential. My suspicions immediately turned to Ms. Conales.

On December 4, 1996, our Group Supervisor, Ivan Winkowsky, posted an email message from Donald Chin, Assistant Special Agent in Charge (ASAIC), on the bulletin board in the entryway of our office for everyone to see. Winkowsky was about a 48-year-old white male, rather simple and unimpressive looking. The message Winkowsky posted stated, "For anyone who is experiencing any problems at the

RAIC/Riverside, the preferred method of reporting problems is by using the chain of command." On the memo hanging on the bulletin board at the RAIC/Riverside someone had written the word "one" on the memo, indicating that there was only one person having a problem at the RAIC/Riverside. I immediately recognized the handwriting as that of the office brown-noser, Edwin Easel.

A cross between the TV character Frank Burns from M*A*S*H* and former Vice President Al Gore, Easel the Weasel, as we commonly referred to him, could not investigate his way out of a paper bag. This didn't matter to Customs management because he was a white male and one of the "good old boys." Easel was of average height and weight and very handsome in an impish sort of way. He spent an inordinate amount of time in Winkowsky's office having cases spoon-fed to him. Unlike Ruben and I, he had no prior law enforcement background and had not successfully completed any significant cases on his own. Winkowsky ate this guy up, buying his brown-nosing act hook, line and sinker. Winkowsky was cut from the same cloth. He moved up in the "Customs Crony System" much in the same way that most white male agents did. It was never about what you did, but who you knew and if you were the right gender and color. This was common knowledge throughout the agency, and Ruben and I naively thought that we could change things.

I was furious when I saw the posted email message. Any anonymity that Ruben should have retained went right out the window. When I showed it to Ruben I sensed that he was both angry and concerned. Ruben was part of a dying breed of hard-core cops. He only revealed the tough cop demeanor on the job, but I have seen this tough guy with his kids, coaching little league, and the softy in him could not help but come out. I have also seen the softer side of Ruben in his concern for my well-being. Ruben and my husband had become fast friends, and they loved to enjoy themselves, jokingly, at my expense. When Ruben and I partnered up and became office cellmates, I could tell that at first, he was leery of working with a woman. It took me a while to earn his respect and trust, but it was certainly worth it.

The next day, when Winkowsky had gone for lunch, I noticed that he had left his checkbook on his desk. I took the next check out of his book, grabbed a quick lunch and waited for his return. I let Bob Mattivi, Acting Group Supervisor, in on the joke I was about to play on Winkowsky. He had complained to us many times about his wife's spending habits. This poor woman always had to either sneak checks from him or to ask his permission to spend money. How Winkowsky treated his wife indicated to me how Winkowsky viewed women and their place in life. Winkowsky could rightfully be called the stereotypical male chauvinist, and this annoyed me. When Winkowsky returned from lunch, I was in the back office where he could not see me. I placed a call to him disguising my voice. I told him that I was from his bank and wanted clearance to use his overdraft protection for the check we had just received for $7,000. He fell for my act, and I could hear him grab his checkbook and thumb through it in a panic. I gave him the check number and told him it was signed by a Pamela Winkowsky (his wife). I told him we normally did not call for overdraft protection, but because it was for such a large amount, and since he had never used his overdraft before, it looked suspicious.

He said frantically, "No, no, I'm not authorizing this." "Well Mr. Winkowsky, I'm not here to ascertain if you gave her permission, sir, only to verify whether or not this is your wife's signature." "Well yeah, but I never authorized this amount." "Well, sir, she is on your joint account, and I was just verifying that she did in fact sign this check. She doesn't need your authorization." Winkowsky was breathing hard. "Just, just hold on a minute, just hold on," and he put me on hold. I walked up the hall just short of his office as he furiously called his wife and cussed her out as he dialed. Bob and I burst out laughing. Winkowsky looked at us laughing in his doorway and caught on to the joke as I waived his check back and forth. Bob took one look at Winkowsky's face and started howling, "Oh Darlene, that was the funniest thing I've ever seen. Oh Dar, that was great; I'm going to have a stroke," he laughed. Winkowsky was furious. He started cussing us both out and we collapsed onto his couch laughing. Then, realizing that his wife had not spent $7,000, he started laughing with us, just a little. That would be the last time I would ever laugh with Winkowsky about anything.

Later that day, I placed the first of many calls to Ms. Conales in an attempt to get information about the class EEO complaint. Although I left numerous messages, she never returned my calls. I was suspicious that she was stringing me along, so I called her secretary and made an appointment.

On December 7, 1996, I took a day off work and drove three hours into Long Beach for my meeting with Ms. Conales. She still claimed not to have the necessary information to instruct me on filing a class EEO complaint. I showed her the email message posted by Winkowsky and she began to squirm. I asked her how it was that SAIC/LA management found out so quickly about Ruben's complaint being filed. She was extremely uncomfortable with my question and told me management must have seen Victor Ross' travel request for the trip from San Diego to Los Angeles. This answer just increased my suspicions. I knew that the travel request for Ross would not have gone through SAIC/LA's management but would have been processed through SAIC/San Diego, the office at which Victor worked. SAIC/LA would not even have a reason to review it.

Ms. Conales once again failed to properly advise me on how to file a class EEO complaint. In fact, she really was no help at all. She assured me again that she would research it and get back to me, but I sensed that something else was behind Ms. Conales' excuses. Several weeks went by, and though I continued to call Ms. Conales, documenting each time I called her, she never returned my calls or provided the information I had requested.

Darlene with Customs Mobile X-ray van

Chapter Four

The "Good Old Boy" System

On December 17, 1996, while scanning radio frequencies, Ruben intercepted a conversation between SA Edwin Easel and recently promoted Supervisory Special Agent (SSA) Peter Blake. They were wrapping up a surveillance in La Verne, California, and neither wanted to travel to RAIC/Riverside to secure the narcotics evidence for the night. As the evidence custodians for our office, they were well aware that this was a major violation of Customs policy, and could sacrifice the whole case based on violation of chain of custody rules/laws. Ruben and I were supporting the case agent, SA Janet Somers, a short, hefty, white woman on this case.

On January 9, 1997, SA Janet Somers officially notified Group Supervisor Ivan Winkowsky that she believed that the heroin involved in her controlled delivery had been taken home on December 17 by one of the evidence custodians instead of being properly placed in the evidence locker until the following morning. Janet was obviously concerned about the upcoming trial on this case and the effect that the break in the chain of custody would have on it. Winkowsky, upon learning of this allegation, made no attempt to report this violation of Customs policy to the Office of Internal Affairs (IA), and instead, chose to cover up this incident, violating Customs policy and federal law. I suspected that Winkowsky would not have covered for anyone in that office except his cronies. Now these "good old boys" would owe him a favor. That is how it works in the Customs Service.

On January 29, 1997, SA Janet Somers was asked to fax her entire case file, including file notes, to Assistant U.S. Attorney (AUSA) Bailey Miller. She went to Winkowsky to reiterate her concerns about the heroin incident. The case file included notes referring to the misconduct by the evidence custodians, Easel and Blake, and Somers was quite certain that she would be questioned about this matter by the AUSA. Janet later told Ruben that at first, Winkowsky denied that he had any knowledge of ever previously discussing this misconduct with her. Then Janet showed him her "9-B, Case Chronology and Review Form" dated January 9, 1997, signed off on by Winkowsky on her quarterly review in which she documented the fact that she had personally made him aware of this alleged misconduct. Upon seeing the document, Winkowsky's memory magically returned. However, following their conversation, Winkowsky once again failed to report the misconduct to IA.

On February 2, 1997, my G-ride , slang for government issued vehicle, needed to go into the shop. Ruben was on leave for a couple of days, so I grabbed the extra keys to his G-ride from the key box. I was shocked to find that the steering was virtually out! I had been training for the 1999 Police Olympics, had extremely good upper body strength, and it was all that I could do just to cut the wheel. When I went to put on the brakes, they, too, were faulty. Ruben had been complaining about this car to Winkowsky for a while, but Winkowsky had refused to issue him another vehicle. I could not believe that Ruben had been driving this!

I parked the car and went back into the office for a different set of keys. The key box was in Winkowsky's office behind his door. As I entered his office, he was sitting at his desk. I just shook my head as I reached for the key box. "What are you doing?" he asked. "I'm getting another car; that piece of crap you got Ruben driving is dangerous, and you're lucky he hasn't gotten hurt." "There's nothing wrong with that car," he said and shooed me out the door. I could feel myself getting angry. I walked over to him, leaned over his desk, and placed my face uncomfortably close to his, glaring into his eyes. I slammed the keys to

Ruben's car down on the desk almost hitting his hand. He was startled and jerked back in an effort to create some distance. My voice was low and cracking with anger as I said, "Be careful Ivan; be careful" and walked out.

I was headed out with most of the rest of the office to one of Easel's surveillances. When I arrived at the debriefing location most of the office, including Renado and a couple of his guys, was there. I high-fived Renado and said, "Hey guys, what are you doing here?" He responded, "Ah you know, the usual; Customs can't handle a case without us, you know that Dar," he laughed. "Someone's got to watch out for you rookies." Weasel briefed us: our primary function was to watch a video store for a certain crook to come out. He gave us a loose description of the crook and said that we were to follow him upon his departure. At the end of the briefing I asked Easel why he did not have a photo of his crook, and he gave a weak excuse.

We had been sitting for a couple of hours when Renado drove up to me and asked, "Hey, Dar, how come we haven't seen anyone coming or going from this store? I mean, is it even open?" I got out of my car and walked past the store. On the front of the door were listed the store hours and a sign stating that the store was closed. I went back to my car and got the acting supervisor, Robert Mattivi, on the radio. Bob was a rather large fellow, white male, about 53 years old and had a heart the size of Wyoming. He was also one of the smartest guys I'd ever met, second only to my husband, Ben. I radioed Bob to meet with me and Renado. By the time Bob arrived, I had already told Renado what I had seen on the door. Renado was laughing and shaking his head when Bob pulled up.

I told Bob what I'd just seen and shared my frustration about Easel's pulling everyone out here on a surveillance of a closed business. Hadn't he done any elementary legwork to obtain a picture of the crook or at least see when the store opened? Renado said, "Bob, where did you get this guy? The K-Mart School of Investigators?" Renado and I burst out laughing. Bob replied, "Hey, this isn't my boy. This is one of Winkowsky's protégés." I stopped laughing, looked at Bob and said, "Bob, buddy, do something about this moron, please. Most of us have real work to do." Bob shook his head and angrily called Easel over the radio and told him to meet with him. Bob was obviously embarrassed for our agency in front of Renado and his San Bernardino Police Department. Bob apologized and sent us all home. As we were leaving and driving past Easel, Renado yelled and pointed to Easel, "Hey, everyone, here's the next Customs GS-13." The thought that this incompetent agent could be promoted over Ruben or me was just sickening. This was not the first time Easel had pulled a bonehead stunt like this and received no punishment from Winkowsky.

Chapter Five

EEO = Frustration

In late February 1997, Ruben asked me if I had filed anything yet. I could sense the concern in his expression. I told him of how, after several calls and a meeting with Ms. Conales, she still had not provided the procedure for filing a class EEO complaint. Ruben instructed me that there was a timeline; if I didn't file my complaint within 45 days, I would be ineligible to file. This was the first time that anyone had informed me of deadlines!

On March 17, 1997, I filed the following individual EEO complaint and faxed it to the head of EEO, Lindsey Watts, in Washington D.C., as well as Ms. Conales.

Dear Ms. Watts,

I am filing this Equal Opportunity complaint with great sadness. I feel that I have exhausted all other means to avoid any kind of formal complaint, to include using my chain of command. I feel that these issues could be resolved informally with proper communication, development of a truly objective/impartial promotion system, and good personnel training for our management.

For the past eight years, my management has treated me very differently, from several of my white, male counterparts. This treatment includes management failing to recommend me for awards on successful cases I have completed, when others are consistently submitted for awards for very similar, and sometime less results. In addition to awards, these same individuals are consistently supported on their cases, and assignments. I feel that this bias behavior of our management also had an effect on the recent GS-13 promotions at our RAIC office.

In August 1996, I talked to our RAIC, James Wilson, about my concerns. As an example of this unfair treatment, I brought to Mr. Wilson's attention one specific case that I put a lot of effort into (Operation Truck Stop) where I was left out completely by my supervisor Ivan Winkowsky when awards were presented. Individuals, who did much less work on this case than I, were presented awards in from of the entire SAC Office. The case agent himself, Robert Mattivi, even fully agreed that the way I was treated was a "real slap in the face." Mr. Wilson agreed that what took place in regards to this case was a mistake and he apologized. After my conversation with Mr. Wilson, the unfair treatment from management subsided for a while. Mr. Wilson retired in December 1994. After Mr. Wilson left, the unfair treatment slowly resumed. In November 1995, another female agent in our office, Millie Landon, complained about very similar issues of gender bias to a member of a Headquarters Inspection Team named Darcy Fields. Millie's supervisor at the time was Allen Casey. As a result of her complaint, she was treated very badly by Mr. Casey.

This blatant retaliation received by my fellow agent, combined with my own concerns about the way I was being treated prompted me to talk to Mr. Antonio Pulaski. Mr. Pulaski was, at that time the ASAIC (Assistant Special Agent In Charge) in charge of the RAIC offices in our area. I told Mr. Pulaski about the concerns of myself, and several other people in our office. I gave him specific examples of unfair treatment where management was engaging in very bias behavior in the areas of awards, schools, and general support on cases. I also warned him that someone would eventually file some type of formal grievance. After my talk with Mr. Pulaski the unfair behavior exhibited by our supervisors stopped. Several months later, Mr. Pulaski left the U.S. Customs Service, and again, the unfair behavior of our management resumed.

In November 1996, Special Agent Ruben Sandoval, RAIC/Riverside, filed an EEO complaint regarding many of the same issues and concerns that I am presenting to you. Through the course of his EEO investigation, I was interviewed by EEO Counselor Victor Ross, San Diego region and by EEO Supervisor Ms. Mary Conales, Los Angeles region. I gave Conales and Mr. Ross many specific examples of the bias[ed] behavior exhibited by our management at RAIC/Riverside.

In addition to many other concerns, I explained to them how my promotion score received by the CAAPS promotion system was much higher than my male counterparts who were promoted over me. I explained to Mr. Ross and Ms. Conales that during the promotion board convened at the SAC office, I gave very clear information to verify that my score was correct. My board consisted of Mr. Donald Chin, Ms. Kelley Lambert, and Mr. Dudley O'Shea. For each case discussed not only did I give them the seizure and arrest information requested, I also provided them with names of prosecutors, DEA supervisors, and other agency case agents who would verify all of my work. I had this information written down on a piece of paper next to the correlating case, and I handed the paper to Mr. Chin. Mr. Chin attempted to give this back to me, and I told him that he could keep it. His lack of interest in verifying my work concerned me greatly.

I further explained to Mr. Ross and Ms. Conales that when the promotion list was released, I telephonically contacted every single person (prosecutors, DEA personnel, case agents) that I had given it in support of my casework. None of them had been contacted by anyone from Customs regarding my cases. This demonstrated to me, a lack of verification of casework.

I gave Conales and Mr. Ross many other examples of bias/unfair behavior exhibited by our management. I also gave her a copy of an email message sent to our office for Ivan Winkowsky to post, and he did. The message was from Donald Chin, and directed that any complaints that individuals have at RAIC/Riverside should be forwarded through the chain of command. This message was in response to Ruben Sandoval's EEO complaint.

I have a real problem with this message. First of all, you will find that no one tried harder to get cooperation from my chain of command regarding these concerns, than me. I come from a military background, and I truly believe in the chain of command. This is why I put up with being treated very unfairly for eight (8) years while I continually attempted to obtain help from my chain of command. I wanted very much for this to be resolved informally, and made every effort to do so. I went to my supervisor, face to face, and told him of my concerns. When that didn't work, I talked to my RAIC Mr. Wilson. I subsequently asked for help from ASAIC Mr. Pulaski. That is, BY DEFINITION, using my chain of command!

The combination of my attempting to get help from my chain of command, and other individuals complaining to the inspection team about management's behavior should have sparked some type of reaction or show of concern from management. This chain of command was the most warned group of people probably in the history of Customs. Most people in our office will tell you that you could see these complaints coming a mile away, and that it could have been easily prevented. I am also aware of other offices where similar grievances have been filed (e.g. Calexico, California).

In spite of the above concerns, I truly am proud of being a Customs Agent. It amazes me that when it comes to other programs/systems in our agency (i.e. Customs computer programs, laboratories, fitness programs), Customs literally runs circles around every other agency. We have the bragging rights about virtually everything in comparison to our fellow state and federal agencies, except when it comes to systems involving our promotions and awards. When it comes to this, we seem to fall on our face. This agency deserves to have the absolute best promotion and awards system possible.

In light of the recent barrage of complaints involving the recent promotions, the Customs service should accept the fact that what we have just isn't working. We should view this as a learning experience, and as a problem that simply needs to be solved. The CAAPS Scoring System was definitely a step in the right direction, and a good one at that. It just seems to me that in many cases local management simply tossed this scoring system right out the window, gave it no credence, and reverted back to their old ways.

We do not have to "reinvent the wheel" here to come up with a better system. There are many promotion and awards systems that are excellent models that could be easily tailored to our agency. I DO NOT want this complaint to simply be a part of the problem. I want very much to be a part of the solution. Instead of reacting to these grievances with a "knee jerk" overreaction, and/or trying to put a Band-Aid on a great gaping, oozing, hole, let's solve the problem. We can do this; I know we can. Any agency that can come up with amazing systems like our computer system, that other agencies truly are jealous of, can certainly come up with a system of promotion and awards that we can also brag about.

This is the point of my complaint. I'm not asking for people to be punished, let's train them instead. I am, however, pleading with Customs Service to take a close look at what we have, and come up with better systems of promotion and awards that we can truly be proud of. When it comes to these issues, there is a severe morale problem among our agents. I am confident that if Customs completed a nation-wide, confidential survey rating it's promotional and awards systems, we would be very depressed at the results.

As I look back on this letter, I realize just how naive I was about how the system operates and what the results of this complaint would be. The EEO counselor assigned to me by Ms. Conales was SA Tam Zodo assigned to the SAIC/LA, California, and working for Drake Brinkley. SA Zodo had just been promoted under the same promotion system that I was complaining about. I later found out from my attorney that I should never have been assigned an EEO counselor from the same chain of command that I was complaining about, and certainly not a white male who was just promoted under that same system that I was disputing.

Several months went by, and SA Zodo never interviewed me. I called numerous times and talked to him twice. Both times he told me he needed to get out here and have me sign some paperwork, but he never showed. Eight months later, and to the shock and dismay of many, we would learn that SA Zodo was facing conviction of shoplifting, fraud, violation of federal firearms laws and money laundering. And this was the type of agent that Brinkley promoted over Ruben and me. No wonder he was too busy to interview me.

Chapter Six

The BQL and EEO: Acronyms with No Ethics

On September 17, 1997, Ruben and I were again up for promotion. Winkowsky was tasked by RAIC Lawrence Evantie to supervise, review and verify all case experience regarding the upcoming GS-13 promotions. Evantie was our new resident office manager for the RAIC/Riverside. He was a tall, skinny, almost nerdy white male with dark greasy hair and glasses. Before he arrived, several of us in the office had heard that he had a reputation for being difficult. He had come from another agency and had basically been promoted through Brinkley's "good old boy system." Evantie, like most Customs managers, was well connected to the "Brinkley Brown-Noser Gang" and had very few successful cases under his belt. I personally talked to several of his peers and subordinates from Arizona, and they all said the same thing: Evantie was an extreme narcissistic jerk who got into management the normal Customs way. Evantie and Winkowsky were cut from the same mediocre government cloth.

As a result of Winkowsky's review, points would be decided by him and forwarded to the Office of Personnel Management (OPM). I had my reservations about Winkowsky's ability to be unbiased and objective. I wrote a memo to Evantie requesting that Winkowsky not be allowed to evaluate the experience of Ruben and I for obvious reasons. My request was denied. Of course, Winkowsky, once again, hammered us on our CAAPS (Customs Automated Assistance Promotion System) scores, but we still made the best qualified list (BQL). My previous CAAPS score, and two subsequent CAAPS scores completed by supervisors other than Winkowsky, were 10 points higher than the one that Winkowsky had given.

On June 3, 1997, I confronted my supervisor, Winkowsky, about the vehicle assignment situation. At the time, I had been driving a car that for several weeks prior to this date was routinely overheating and dying. The car had over 125k miles, and the air-conditioning was no longer working. Under other circumstances, air-conditioning might be considered a luxury, but our surveillances and controlled deliveries were often in or around Indio, California (the desert), in very high temperatures during the months of June and July. Here it was seen as a necessity.

I noticed on this surveillance that SSA Jerry Johnston was driving a new car. His previous vehicle only had 94k miles, was not dying or overheating, had air-conditioning, and to my knowledge, was in good operating order. When I asked Winkowsky why Jerry had been given a new vehicle when I clearly needed one, he replied, "Mr. Brinkley directed that Jerry's truck be turned in and he be assigned a new vehicle."

I later asked Jerry about this and he said all he knew was that Brinkley had ordered it. When I told Jerry about my car situation, I could tell that he felt badly for me and didn't want there to be any hard feelings. I assured him that I knew this was not his doing and that everything was cool. Jerry was a soft-spoken, handsome, white male with dark hair and eyes. He had a distinctive, ultra-professional military aura about him. Jerry and I were kindred spirits. We were the only agents in the office who were prior military officers. Jerry Johnston was a good man and an excellent criminal investigator. He believed, as I did, and as we were both taught, that the mission comes first, then your men, and lastly yourself. We both found later that this was not the philosophy of the Department of Treasury.

On June 6, 1997, as I walked into the office, Winkowsky stopped me in the hall and asked that I come into the office of Yolanda Rios, our office administrator. Yolanda was a dark-skinned, short haired, very pretty Puerto Rican woman. Her demeanor was direct, forward and very outspoken. She had a great sense of humor and always talked with her hands. Yolanda's attitude helped give the workplace a pleasant atmosphere.

Winkowsky seemed very nervous and had a "slippery" demeanor about him. He told me that an EEO investigator, Orlando Lopez, was here to interview people regarding Ruben Sandoval's case. Winkowsky also told me that new cars were coming into the SAIC office and that I would be getting one. I couldn't believe what I was hearing. He was attempting to soften up my testimony by bribing me with a car! I shook my head in disgust and said skeptically, "Sure, Ivan, sure." Any respect I had left for the man disintegrated. I found myself surprised and disgusted at his fear and willingness to sink to such levels. I went into the meeting with Lopez and told the truth, pulling no punches.

On August 5, 1997, I contacted Conales and brought to her attention the negligence of the EEO counselor she had assigned me. She immediately assigned me a new EEO counselor, Senior Inspector Anna Francisco. August 1997 was the first time that I actually met with an EEO counselor. I asked around about Francisco, and the feedback I received was very good. She was known to be a very good inspector and a well-respected EEO counselor. I met with Francisco at our RAIC office where she explained to me my EEO rights and laid out a timeline of deadlines. She even had an EEO rights form that she filled out for me describing my EEO rights. During our meeting, I could not help but wonder why Conales had failed to advise me of any of this.

On December 12, 1997, I gave Francisco all of my documentation to date. This documentation included a sworn statement written by SA Sandy Nunn in support of both Ruben and me. Sandy Nunn and I had been friends since we first entered Customs ten years earlier. She was a cute, tiny blond who had a real spark of life in her eyes. The two of us were often endearingly referred to as the "Glitter Girls." This nickname had as much to do with our wardrobes as it did anything else. Sandy and I were known to dress a lot more "up-scale" than the average agent. We were both clothes hounds. My husband often referred to us as the "Emelda Marcos" agents. Between the two of us, we could fill up a warehouse with shoes and clothes. Sandy had been assigned to the SAIC/LA office and was a brilliant agent, the case agent on the famous "L.A. Jewelry Mart Case." This case was a huge international money laundering case written up in *Newsweek* and was one of Customs' most successful cases ever. Sandy was no slouch as an agent, and I had tremendous respect for her.

When I read the statement Sandy had offered to me, I was very impressed, but I also expressed my concerns regarding the impending doom that I felt would follow as the result of her statement. This was going to infuriate Brinkley, and I warned her to be ready to accept the consequences of a possible transfer. She bravely plowed forward in disbelief of my prediction. I was very proud of her courage. The following is the professional, eloquent, and truthful statement written by Sandy Nunn:

> Since October 1988, I have been employed with the U.S. Customs Service in Los Angeles, California in the capacity of a Special Agent. During this 9-year period, I have been assigned to the Office of the Special Agent in Charge located on Terminal Island. As a long-standing employee in this office, I have had the opportunity to actively observe the overall morale, conduct, general health and well-being of the employee base, daily happenings, politics, and so forth of all personnel assigned to this office. This has afforded me the unique position to draw certain comparisons with regard to each of the five (5) areas outlined above.

> When I arrived at the SAIC/LA in October 1988, I observed that employee morale was extremely high. Employees were happy, enthusiastic about their work, motivated, and felt very

relaxed in their dealings with upper management. I observed during that time that management appeared to care a great deal about the employees as individuals and that an "open door policy" was encouraged to make it easier for employees to address concerns. This attitude made employees feel more comfortable. Subsequently, for the most part, employee health and well-being appeared to be very optimum since stress levels were low. As a result of a positive work atmosphere, productivity was at an all-time high.

Contrasting that picture with the SAIC/LA today, I observe an office in which employee morale is dangerously low, happiness is non-existent, enthusiasm and motivation has been severely curbed contributing to low productivity levels, and stress has replaced relaxed feelings to the degree that several agents have had to go out on stress leave or have had to resort to taking anti-depressant medications such as Prosaic. Further, U.S. Customs is losing experienced agents who feel they have no choice but to leave early either through early retirement or by switching agencies. I have also observed an onslaught of stress-related disorders among my fellow agents consisting of headaches, inability to eat or sleep, feelings of frustration and anger, even suicidal thoughts. Further exacerbating the problem is what I perceive as a strong tendency on the part of management to micromanage the work of the agents of this office by engaging in lengthy case review meetings, playing definite favorites with certain agent personnel to the exclusion of others with regard to how cases and/or other assignments are to be divided and carried out, and by engaging in favoritism with regard to promotions. Most significant of all is an attitude by management, which I would term "management by threat." There is a definite attitude by management of this office that the way to keep the agents under control is to threaten and

intimidate them into submission. This is very common knowl-
edge among everyone in this office and it takes place very
openly and to such degree that I have actually witnessed per-
sonality changes in agents I have worked with for many years.
Further, agents who I know to be highly competent and mature
have actually openly expressed feelings of fear toward manage-
ment. This is due to the fact that there are many examples of
productive agents who have been intimidated, threatened, and
harassed by upper management over a period of time in this
office, as well as throughout the entire Customs Service.
Coming from a highly educated background in the field of
electronics engineering and having served in the corporate
world prior to my employment with U.S. Customs, I find this
management style very inappropriate and highly contributory
to what is termed under law as a hostile working environment.
In point of fact, this behavior is illegal under federal laws and
should not be tolerated.

Therefore, I am making this statement of my own free will
based upon my observations into these matters. Further, by
making this statement and signing my complete name, I am
hereby designating myself as a "whistleblower" as defined under
the Whistleblower Act with all the protections accorded me
under this law.

SANDRA G. NUNN
Special Agent
U.S. Customs Service

On January 8, 1998, when Anna Francisco finished her EEO investi-
gation, she put her report, which included Sandy's statement, on the
desk of EEO supervisor, Ms. Mary Conales. On January 12, 1998, Drake
Brinkley signed a memo ordering that Sandy Nunn be transferred.

Sandy called and explained what had happened. She was distraught and on the verge of tears. When her boss called her into his office to break the news to her, he told her that he himself had just found out. Sandy was being transferred to the DEA Technical Task Force in downtown Los Angeles. In our agency, this was commonly referred to as the dumping ground. Everyone knew that was where management sent all the people they perceived as "problem agents." When Sandy walked out of her supervisor's office, she saw the Customs Task Force Coordinator, Fred Lauder, walking out of the weekly office management meeting. When he entered the hall she walked up to him and said, "Hi, I hear that I'm going to be working for you starting next week." Lauder was taken by surprise as he had no idea Sandy was being transferred to his group. We found this most interesting since this was not how normal transfers worked. Supervisors are always advised well in advance of any personnel changes being made. Two days after SAIC Brinkley signed the transfer memo for Sandy Nunn, Brinkley signed another memo addressed to all agents at the SAIC/LA. This memo stated:

> With the expected influx of new personnel in the next 6 months there is a need to place them where they will be the most effective for the Office of Investigations. In an effort to get a better understanding of the background and experience level of current SAIC/LA agents within the immediate commuting distance of Terminal Island, LAX and RAIC/OR, please advise me of the following information for each agent within your chain of command. Please submit this info on all 1811 personnel to Associate SAIC Woody Pillsbury by February 1. Thank you.

> 1. Time as a Customs Special Agent?

> 2. Time in present group/office?

> 3. Time spent in Terminal Island, RAIC/LX, and RAIC/OR?

> 4. Investigative disciplines worked?

5. Office/group in which you would most desire to work within the SAC/LA?

6. Would you desire a tour in Headquarters?

Drake Brinkley

This memo basically allowed all agents of the SAIC/LA to have input as to whether or not they would like to be transferred and where. Everyone, that is, except Sandy Nunn. Sandy's transfer memo was obviously a knee-jerk reaction to something, most likely Sandy's letter, which was supposed to remain anonymous. The only way management could have known about this was from Conales. If she leaked this information to management, then it would be a clear violation of Sandy's rights and a violation of the Privacy Act and the Whistleblower Act. I knew instinctively that Conales had betrayed us.

I called Francisco and told her what had happened to Sandy. She, too, was outraged and very concerned. She later confronted Conales about the situation and was fired shortly thereafter by Conales from her position as an EEO counselor. She was devastated. She called me with this news and could not restrain her tears. Sandy filed an EEO retaliation complaint based upon what had happened to Francisco.

On March 2, 1998, Ms. Conales lied in a sworn statement alleging that in our December 1996 meeting at her office in Long Beach, I had not requested counseling on particular issues affecting me and that she had made me aware of what the EEO process entailed. When I read this I was furious. What did she think I drove three hours one way to her office for; to have lunch? Subsequently, my EEO complaint was denied by the Regional Complaint Center based on timeliness. Conales had strung me along, not notifying me of any timelines, and built in a standard excuse for my complaint to be denied. I later learned that these were routine tactics for her. She did this to Ervin Rios, Ruben, Sandy and numerous others. There was a definite, well-documented pattern here, if only someone cared enough to look. But, of course, no one did. It was obvious that Conales was in bed with Customs management.

On March 26, 1998, Sandy and I met with Jay Rosden, Port Director in Lukeville, Arizona. The purpose of our meeting was for Sandy to file an EEO retaliation report for her forced transfer. I arrived at the lobby of the Hilton before Sandy, at approximately 1030hrs. After she arrived we met with Mr. Rosden. Nearly five hours later, with our interviews not yet finished, I received a page from my Acting Group Supervisor, David Gray. Gray was a very nerdy, unattractive, balding white male. He was a stereotypical computer geek, complete with pocket protector and wired rimmed glasses. When I called Gray back, he asked where I was and what I was doing. He sounded stressed. I asked if he had gotten my voicemail messages, and he said he had. He told me that Evantie wanted to know what was going on. I answered that this was regarding my EEO issue. Then, in a pathetic attempt at intimidation he said, "Well, what issue? I mean, is this something new or what?" I replied, "Well, why don't you speak to the EEO counselor yourself?" and I handed the phone to Mr. Rosden.

As I handed it to him, he had a look of slight panic on his face. I felt a little guilty for passing the buck to Rosden in order to evade being grilled further and to get out of a very inappropriate situation. Mr. Rosden seemed to be a very capable man and a good supervisor, a rarity in Customs. He got on the phone, and at first it was clear that he was talking to Gray. Then the conversation changed, and I could tell by the use of Lawrence's name that Mr. Rosden was now talking to RAIC Evantie. At the very beginning of the conversation, SA Arnold Connez, SAIC/LA, walked up to us in the lobby and witnessed the conversation. It was very apparent that Mr. Rosden was being "interrogated" by Evantie. In return, Rosden was attempting to be polite, yet evasive, about Evantie's questions. The poor man was squirming. Sandy and I had not yet filled out any paperwork or had the opportunity to inform

Mr. Rosden whether or not we wanted to remain anonymous regarding this issue.

When Mr. Rosden got off the phone, the look on his face was one of disbelief. He told us that he was very uncomfortable about the way that had been handled. We finished our interviews at approximately 1700hrs. I knew traffic would be horrendous due to the rain and rush hour, so I decided to wait out the traffic and grab something to eat. I departed for home at approximately 1900hrs.

As I was driving up the street to my house around 2100hrs, I got another page from Gray at our office in Riverside. I went into the house and returned his call. He started the conversation by attempting to put me on speakerphone. Given what I already knew of Gray, I suspected he was doing this because he wanted someone else to listen to our conversation, most likely Evantie. At no time did Gray have the common courtesy to ask my permission to put me on speakerphone or allow someone else to listen to our conversation. I was livid. He tried several times to engage the speakerphone but was unable to get it to work. I did find it a bit humorous that he could not even use the speaker device on the phone!

He told me that the purpose for his call was to see if I was all right. "That's bull–!" I thought to myself. Then he asked me a string of questions: "Why are you just now getting home? Why did it take so long?" I explained to him that because of the rain, it took me three hours to get from my house to Long Beach this morning and the interviews just lasted longer than expected. I further explained that I did not want to fight rush-hour traffic coming back, so I stayed to eat and left Long Beach at about 1900hrs and had just arrived home.

"Lawrence just wanted to know what was going on, and why you were gone so long," he said. He continued on in an official tone of voice as though he was performing for someone. "The EEO counselor should have contacted Riverside management and made arrangements to conduct the interviews at the RAIC/Riverside Office. The EEO counselor was out of line by not doing so." "I feel that what took place on the phone with Evantie 'grilling' the EEO counselor was very inappropriate," I responded. Gray said, "Lawrence has every right to know that information, so it wasn't inappropriate." We politely argued the point, as if both of us feared that we were being recorded or watched. I informed Gray that there were three people who witnessed the conversation between the EEO counselor and Evantie. There was dead silence, and I could sense Gray cringing on the other side of the phone.

I told him that Mr. Rosden had expressed to Sandy and me that he was very uncomfortable about the conversation and agreed with me that it was inappropriate. Gray responded that the EEO counselor should have never said that and assured me that the EEO counselor would be in very big trouble with his management if they knew he had. "The EEO counselor did not need to tell us how uncomfortable he was, Gray; it was painfully apparent that the man was almost squirming, he was so uncomfortable. We saw the obvious for ourselves." Gray changed the topic back to the reason for his phone call: it was just to make sure that I was OK and had made it home safely. This was such a joke. In 11 years of being an agent, going out on surveillances and deals where I returned in the middle of the night, no one in Customs had ever called to see if I got home OK—no one!

After I hung up with Gray, I again felt that this contact by management was out of line. If management had a problem with the way Mr. Rosden was conducting himself, then Gray and Evantie should have been on the phone with Mr. Rosden expressing these views, not with me. I knew that the real purpose of the late phone call was just another fishing expedition about this EEO matter which, at this point, was none of his business. Gray was just doing Evantie's dirty work for him.

After my conversation with Gray, my phone rang. It was Sandy. I told her what had just happened and suggested that we call Mr. Rosden. Sandy placed a three-way call to Mr. Rosden and we told him what had just transpired, including Gray's comment about his being in trouble. I apologized to Mr. Rosden if I had gotten him into any trouble, and he assured me that everything was alright. I again shared my feelings about how out of line both telephone conversations were. I explained to him that I thought it inapproriate that I was caught in the middle. He agreed. Sandy and I were both livid. I had a hard time sleeping that night and had a feeling that something odious about to happen.

Chapter Seven

Operation Railroad Begins

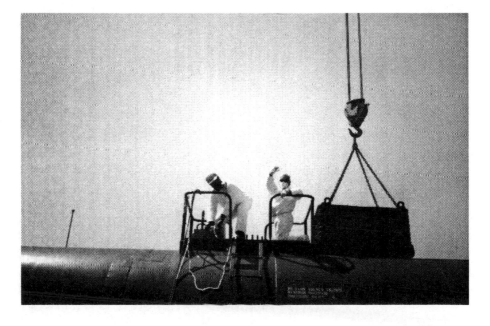

Darlene on top of rail tanker car with drug seizure

On April 7, 1998, Gray called me into his office. He asked me if I still had my rail project up and running and I told him I did. He informed me that he had just taken a call from inspectors at Calexico. Four days prior they had sent a series of tanker cars to Union Pacific to be weighed, and they would be up next week to check them. "Next week! We will lose border search authority if we wait that long. Those idiots don't know what they are doing." "Can you handle it?" Gray asked. I could sense Gray's concern. We go way back and used to be close confidants. Then Gray joined IA and changed. He said he was concerned because I had been fighting a bug for several months now. I was struggling because I had also begun my training for the 1999 Police Olympics. For the past couple of days I had been running a low grade fever, had trouble breathing and was losing my voice.

I grabbed the note, and as I was walking back to my office, Gray laughed and said "Choo, choooo." This was a reminder of a prior embarrassment involving a tanker car caper that everyone commonly referred to as the Geraldo Rivera Tanker Car Caper, a reference to when talk-show host Geraldo Rivera opened the tomb of a mobster on national TV, and it was empty. I ignored Gray and put a call in to my contact with the UP Rail Police, SA Tom Best. Tom and I had been working together on rail projects off and on for about six years. He was a great guy and knew more about the railroad than anyone I had ever met. He was an older white male with a big smile and a balding head. He reminded me of a picture of a railroad conductor I had seen on the cover of a children's book. If you put Tom in a conductor's hat and a pair of overalls, he'd be a dead ringer for that picture. I asked him about the cars, and he responded disgustedly, "Yeah, they're here, all 20 of them, clogging up my yard. Can you help me out with this, Darlene?" I told him I was on my way.

As I drove there, I couldn't help thinking about the embarrassing episode that Gray was "choo-chooing" at me over. About five years back, I pegged a car as suspicious because of the way it was imported and the shenanigans that had taken place at the Calexico, California port of entry where the Customs hold was released. Before I had arranged for it to go, it traveled to Colton, California. This put the car in the rail yard on New Years Eve. In addition, on the trip up from Calexico, the railcar was mysteriously unaccounted for for 9 to 12 hours. Nobody could figure out where it had been during this time frame. I was the duty agent that night and had already gotten a call from my comrade, Ervin Rios (no relation to Yolanda Rios, Riverside Investigative Aid), on a suspected load of opium coming through Ontario Airport, UPS (United Parcel Service). I was at UPS attempting to arrange for a controlled delivery of the seizure to Redding, California, when I got the call from Tom Best. He started off the conversation in a coy tone of voice. "Do you know where your railcar is?" "Why Best? You gonna tell me that it isn't sittin' where it's supposed to be?" "Nope…it's heerrreee," Best said, singing it like the kid from the movie "Poltergeist."

I had my hands full trying to arrange a controlled delivery of opium with Customs agents out of San Francisco. It was a hard task given that most agents would rather ring in the New Year with a party than with casework. I ended up making arrangements with the State Bureau of Narcotics Enforcement instead of my own agency for the controlled delivery. Ed Saite, head of security with UPS, let us deliver the package on one of his planes.

I had a little time before the UPS crew and I left on the controlled delivery, so I met Best over at the rail yard. Sure enough, there was our car sitting in the yard. Best made arrangements for the car to be weighed and placed on a bad order (routed to a side track where cars go for repair) so that it would not be moved until I could deal with it the next day.

I pulled another all-nighter on a separate controlled delivery of seized opium that Ervin had made. Ervin was a Latino male of average height and weight, but he was anything but average when it came to the job. The man was brilliant, and stacked up seizures one after another. I donned a UPS uniform, flew to Redding and delivered the package. We ended up seizing 18 pounds of opium and arresting two guys. It made the local papers as a record seizure of opium.

Ervin had just won a fight against Customs for wrongful firing. He had been off of work for over a year and had been financially devastated by it. At the time of his firing, Ervin was working at the Los Angeles International Airport (LAX), and was about to complete a money transport over to the Customs office vault. His partner was a woman named Sarah Brooks. As Ervin was pulling out of the LAX parking lot in his POV (Privately Owned Vehicle), a carload of Mexican males crashed into him. This accident was clearly not Ervin's fault. They all got out of the car, and Ervin attempted to get information from them. None of them would produce any identification, and by their appearance and the appearance of their vehicle, Ervin deduced that they were probable "wet-backs," a slang term for illegal aliens. The driver of the car offered Ervin fifty bucks for the damage, and Ervin took it knowing that he would never see these guys again. If he had not taken the fifty bucks, he would have ended up with nothing. When Ervin returned to the Customs office, he briefed his supervisor and reported the incident to Internal Affairs according to agency policy, a mistake he would later regret.

This type of thing happens a hundred times a day in southern California and numerous times to dozens of Customs Agents. A fender-bender occurs on the freeway with small damage and cash is exchanged in order to avoid insurance increases; no big deal. But, for some unexplained reason, IA went after Ervin like he'd robbed a bank, and eventually they fired him for it. No one could believe it. Both Ruben and I testified on Ervin's behalf, and the Department of Treasury's grievance system later declared it a wrongful firing and gave Ervin back his job. Still, no one from Customs was disciplined in any way for Ervin's wrongful firing. There was no justice or consequences for all of the anguish and hardship dealt to Ervin by Internal Affairs. We had all been in disbelief of the whole situation.

The day after I completed my controlled delivery, I started tackling the logistical nightmare of dealing with the tanker car. I got about three hours of sleep, sucked down an ocean of coffee and Mountain Dew and headed over to the rail yard. When I walked into the UP police station, Best was sitting there laughing hysterically. This was not a good sign. "OK, Best, where is it now?" He responded, "The real question you should be asking is how did it get there." The car had been on an outbound, about to exit the yard. Thank goodness he had caught it.

Rios, the computer whiz, looked up this car and found that the UP computer system, the Eddie Star System, showed that someone from Customs had released the hold. I chalked it up to stupidity and laziness. Little did I know what I had stumbled into.

We arranged for the car to be moved to the GATX (General American Tanker Car Company) facility about a mile away so that it could be safely entered. On the following Tuesday we started burning off the excess fuel from the bottom of the car, a process known as bleeding, in preparation for safely opening the car. As a precaution, we have to notify the fire department before we crack open these cars for fear of a possible booby trap. Crooks have been known to booby trap large loads of narcotics to keep them from being stolen. However, in this instance, some genius from the fire department had leaked it to the press. On Tuesday, the hill overlooking the GATX yard was full of media. Needless to say, when we cracked it open, it was empty. I felt just like Geraldo Rivera when he opened the Mafia mobster's tomb in front of the world on national TV only to find nothing. For weeks everyone called me Geraldo and made choo-choo noises when they walked past me. As I relived this unfortunate memory, I couldn't help but laugh.

Back on my current case, I was on the way to the yard, I called Renado (Sgt. Detective prior narcotics and head of San Bernardino Police Department's Intelligence Section) for some help with a narcotics dog. As soon as I mentioned a railcar, Renado started laughing and saying, "choo-choo." "Ha, Ha, real funny, now get over here and find me a dog, and this time, Einstein, find me a real dog, not just some stray from the pound." On the last embarrassing tanker car episode, Renado supplied a stupid dog that alerted himself almost to death over an empty car.

When I got there, Best had already placed the car on a bad order (the computer listing of the placement of damaged railcars) and had the Haz-Mat team there. Dennis Bar, with UP Haz-Mat, Edmundo, the foreman from GATX, and Ervin Rios were also there. I climbed on top with my cutting sheers and removed the Customs seal on the man-way hatch cover. I bagged and tagged the seal for evidence. Edmundo and Bar lifted the hatch cover exposing the bolts to the hatch-port containing the pressure valves. We immediately noticed that the bolts holding the hatch-port were hand painted white, like with an artist's paintbrush. I looked down at Ervin and said, "What the hell?!" I motioned with my head for Ervin to climb on top. Ervin sighed. He didn't like climbing on top of these cars, but he came up anyway. None of us had ever seen this type of painting before. It was not consistent with normal shop-style painting. I smiled at Ervin, and we both smiled at Best. I said to Edmundo and Bar, "Let's pressure test it."

At my request, they moved the car to another location, out of sight of the media. I was determined not to have another "Geraldo Rivera" episode. As we began the pressure test, we had yet another surprise: negative pressure. When we opened the valve, we heard a distinct sucking sound and no air exited or registered on the outside gage for several minutes. This car had been vacuumed sealed. There was no legitimate commercial purpose for vacuum sealing a pressurized tanker car. In fact, it creates a safety hazard if the car is loaded with certain volatile commodities. About this time, Renado pulled up with a dog. I told Renado what we had, and he was clearly excited. He had the car inspected several times by the narcotics detection dog, but the dog did not alert. I looked at Renado and said, "Another pound puppy, Renado?"

I made a call to Gray, who was the acting group supervisor at the time, and told him what we had. He said he was on his way. When Gray arrived, I briefed him on how these cars worked and why these indicators—the bolts painted white, the car manifested as empty and the port of origin—were so significant. Rios was already working his magic on the Customs computer system. This system, known as ACS, was able to track all imports in the country. Rios pulled the entries on the car and brought it to the site. The car was manifested as a return empty, and had been exported back to the U.S. from a company called Grassa, based in Sinnaloa, Mexico. Grassa is Spanish for oil. I asked Best to set the car up to be weighed and told him to hump it at least three times to ensure an accurate reading. This procedure involves rolling the car down hill allowing gravity to carry it over a hump with the scales.

It took most of the day to manipulate the tanker car back through the yard, one of the largest rail yards in the U.S., to have it weighed. While this was occurring, Gray was on the phone with the "powers that be" pleading for the authorization and funds to pop our car open. I was on the phone to Assistant United States Attorney (AUSA) Yvette Palazuelos. Yvette was our federal prosecutor on several of our Title III's (wire tap investigations) while I was on the HIDTA (High Intensity Drug Trafficking Area) Group 50, task force. I really admired Yvette. She was a cute, tiny, Latina woman, even smaller than me, and a real go-getter. She reminded me of Mighty Mouse. I briefed her on what we had on the case so far and of the time that had elapsed. I had pulled from the UP computer the route the car had taken and gave good reasons for an extended border search. She agreed and granted me extended border search authority, authority only granted to U.S. Customs, which authorizes searches of people, possessions, vehicles, and commodities entering the U.S.

The tanker car weighed in at almost 9000 pounds, which was over the manufacturers scheduled lightweight for this type of pressurized car. Gray, via telephone, authorized me to have the car moved to the GATX facility while we waited for authorization to pop it open. Gray and I were now convinced that the car was loaded. Up pulled Gray, and Evantie and I briefed him. I suggested that from this point on, in order to maintain good border search authority and to provide security, we should have the tanker car guarded until it was opened. Gray agreed and told me that it was probably going to be tomorrow afternoon before they got authorization and funding to have it opened. This was fine, as it would take several hours to move it to the GATX facility anyway. I made it clear to Edmundo, the GATX foreman, that I wanted this car out of sight from both the public and the media. I reminded him of the last "Geraldo Rivera" episode. I didn't want a repeat performance.

Chapter Eight

The Dream

That night I sat in my G-ride baby-sitting the tanker car. I missed tucking in my kids again, and I longed to hold them, kiss them and hear them tell me all about their day in their cute little voices. I called and spoke to each one of them, and hugged and kissed them on the phone, but it wasn't the same. I envied my husband, Ben, for choosing a more normal career in private industry. I dozed off and began to dream. It was the same dream again; this would be the seventeenth time. When I first started having this dream, it scared me to death. I thought it was some type of warning about danger to my kids. Now, after having had it so many times, I was more curious than afraid. Each time the dream took me to a different place, but the dream was always the same. This time I was taken to the town I grew up in: Dayton, Kentucky. I was standing in the street in front of my home. A small boy, about two years old, was stumbling down the street towards me, crying, shaking and dirty. I ran to the child and picked him up. Holding him tightly, I took him into the house and began to bathe him. I tried to get him to talk to me, but he would not. He was so beautiful; he had eyes like the ocean that saw straight through me. I began washing him and noticed that the filth would not come off. I scrubbed to get the grime off, but to no avail. The more I tried, the more despairing and heart-broken I became. The child just stared at me, begging with his eyes for help. His eyes welled up with tears, and I felt like I was dying inside because I wasn't able to separate him from the filth.

Just then a loud crash startled me awake, and I went for my gun. I realized it was just the railcars bumping together as they were being hooked up. My rapid breathing slowed, and I secured my firearm. I then realized that I had had the dream again, and I began to worry about whether it was a premonition of something about to happen, or if I was simply losing my mind. I had three hours left on my shift and just wanted to go home to my family. I thought of the millions of times that I was so tired I just wanted to resign and go home. But I was afraid that I couldn't make it as a regular person. Being a criminal investigator was all I knew; it had been my whole world all of my adult life. As a child I dreamed of being an undercover policewoman as I watched "Charlie's Angels." If I wasn't a federal agent, then who was I? I was sure that I lacked the courage to succeed in another profession. Still, this dream was becoming more frequent, more haunting, and raising my curiosity about dreams to new levels.

Chapter Nine

The Load

It ended up taking two days to bleed out the fumes and clear the tanker car with Haz-Mat. Along with Haz-Mat's Dennis Bar, David Gray and Ruben Sandoval decided I should be the one to make the entry. I agreed and they suited me up in the Haz-Mat costume, making me look like an astronaut. I really didn't want to do this. I was still sick and running a fever, and my ears had been ringing for a couple of weeks. When they turned on the oxygen in my mask, I knew that the mix was too rich, but the technician rigging me up paid no attention to my complaints. They rigged a tripod on top of the car and lowered me down on a rope through the man-way port. It was pitch black inside, and I was trying to hold a spotlight and a video camera. As I was being lowered through the man-way, I cracked my helmet on the edge, and the helmet fell to the bottom. I remember feeling light headed and giggling about the whole event. I was certain that the oxygen mix was too rich, but at this point, I didn't care. As I was being lowered, I could see large packages piled up at both ends—lots of them. I was thrilled! I knew we had hit a big load. As I reached the bottom, I was stumbling around tripping over packages of weed and cocaine. In the process of trying to video the contents of the car, I dropped my light. It was difficult enough to see with the face-mask, and when the light went out it was pretty claustrophobic. I tried to control my breathing, but I felt myself hyperventilating. They had a radio transmitter in the mask, and I heard Bar yelling, "Hey, are you all right? Are you all right?" I answered "Yes," but told them to get me out. As I reached the top, I felt really woozy and nauseous.

I immediately started tearing at my facemask to get it off. Bar said, "Woah, hold it, hold it; calm down, we're getting it off of you." They got my mask off, and I felt like I was on an elevator ride experiencing that sinking feeling. I was very weak and sleepy. Bar examined the O^2 regulator and I heard him say, "Well, no wonder you were having problems; they set your O^2 too rich for your weight." I looked over at the technician who set my regulator and with disdain said, "You stupid clown, I told you it was too rich." He looked embarrassed and turned away. All I wanted to do was lay down and go to sleep, but I noticed everyone down on the ground watching me, waiting for a report, so I stood and gave everyone a big thumbs up.

Everyone started high-fiving, and I climbed down off the car. I got out of the suit, and Ruben, Ervin, Jerry Johnston and Renado gave me hugs and congratulations. I told them how much was in there, and they were pleased. As I sat there trying to regulate my breathing and holding back the appearance of wanting to vomit and pass out, people kept coming up and congratulating me. I looked over at Lawrence Evantie, and he was glaring at me. He walked over and said, "Well Darlene, are you just going to sit there, or are you going to arrange for a controlled delivery?" He pointed as his watch and said, "The clock's ticking." I looked back at him and mumbled under my breath, "You s-o-b, you can't stand this, can you?" Then I stood up and replied, "I'll see to it, sir."

I went to the GATX restroom and tried to throw-up. I hadn't eaten anything all day so all I could manage was the dry heaves. My ears were ringing louder and louder. I splashed water on my face and went back out to the car. I briefed AUSA Yvette and set up the logistics for a controlled delivery to a lumber yard on Mill Street in San Bernardino. SSA Bob Mattivi took over carrying out of the logistics of the controlled delivery. Ruben worked with Renado in getting us bodies for surveillance for the next few days, while Gray took over the bagging and tagging of evidence.

Darlene in Haz-Mat suit ready to make entry into a rail tanker car

At this point I had been awake for almost 30 hours straight, and Gray, Renado, Ruben and Mattivi knew I was fading fast. They ordered me to go home and get some rest so that I would be ready for the delivery tomorrow. I didn't argue. The seizure ended up being 8000 pounds of marijuana and 34 kilos of cocaine. I was so burned out, I didn't even feel anything when they told me. I just wanted to go home, but I was afraid to drive home for fear of falling asleep at the wheel. I stopped and got a highly caffinated Mountain Dew and guzzled it down on an empty stomach. That was not my brightest move. By the time I got home, I felt sick. In an attempt to relieve the sickness, I drank some milk and went to see my kids. They were fast asleep. I kissed them and covered them up. I sat on the floor watching my youngest sleep while I drank my milk. He looked so peaceful and beautiful. I wondered, as I often did lately, if I was being a good mother and if I was doing the best thing for them. As I was sinking into a deep sleep, it hit me; the tanker car wasn't empty. I am not Geraldo Rivera. I am not Geraldo Rivera! I slept well.

At 0600hrs the following morning, Saturday, I got a call from Gray. He asked me if I was up to starting on the federal anticipatory search warrant. "I've already got it written in my head," I told him. "Well, bring your head and your fingers in so that you can type this up." "No problem," I responded. My husband was lying next to me and asked, "Gotta go back to work, babe?" "Sorry, honey," I replied, "we had a big night last night." Ben hugged me and congratulated me on my seizure. I told him about Evantie's attitude towards me after that, and he said, "He's just mad because you're showing up his boys, and that's not supposed to happen. Just blow him off." As I got up, Ben went downstairs and fixed me breakfast. He saw that I was still sick and scolded me for not making an appointment with the doctor. He made me promise to go on Monday. As I sat down to eat breakfast with him, I realized just how lucky I was to have such a wonderful and supportive husband. I wanted to tell him about the dream, but I was afraid of what he would think of me. Again, I kept it to myself.

Seizure of narcotics inside of rail tanker car

Darlene with large seizure of narcotics taken from rail tanker car

I worked on the warrant and met with the appropriate authorities at the railroads and San Bernardino Police Department. The office was a buzz with everyone working together to run down leads. The FBI arrived, trying to lay claim to our case. Typical FBI—wanting you to give them all of your information, yet refusing to share anything of theirs. Unfortunately for them, they had nothing, and we had every-thing; the turf war was on. I got a hold of Yvette and gave her a heads-up on the impending turf war. She told me not to worry. I had a verbal altercation with the FBI agent who had done some undercover work on the front company, the phony private corporation set up to mask illegal activities, that had leased this tanker car. I saw right through the FBI agent's bull and wasn't exactly polite to him. Eventually, they left.

Chapter Ten

The Scare of My Life

On Monday morning I went to the doctor's again. This was the third time I had been in three months, and they still weren't helping me. Because of the ringing in my ears, I was referred to an ear, nose and throat specialist down the hall. There I was given a hearing test and had blood work done. After all of the tests, the doctor informed me that he was mildly concerned because I had several symptoms that matched Multiple Sclerosis (MS). When I heard this, my arms, legs and face felt numb, and my chest got tight. He told me that he was scheduling me for an MRI on Thursday afternoon.

I went back to the office in a total daze. I immediately started worrying about how my husband and kids, not to mention myself, would handle this if I had MS. I had just sat down when I heard Gray yell for Ruben and I to come into his office. He told us that Attorney General Janet Reno had asked for a daily briefing on my case. It seems that this was the first case involving a controlled delivery of narcotics using a railcar. Gray, clearly displeased, began firing off questions about the FBI's related case. I softly interrupted him with the news that I had just received from the doctor. Gray was taken aback. He was on the verge of chewing Ruben and me out, and I broke his rhythm. Ruben's face dropped with concern, and he ignored Gray's insensitive attempts to continue asking questions. Ruben started asking me questions about my doctor's visit. Gray was agitated that he had lost control of his little meeting. He asked me a question, and Ruben answered it for me. Gray fired back at Ruben, "Let her answer her own questions! What are you, her attorney?" Ruben's face got red, and his cheek twitched. I braced myself, preparing to jump in between them. I looked at Ruben so he could see with my facial expressions what I was thinking: let it go, calm down. He took a deep breath, looked at me and said, "Are you all right?" I felt my eyes welling up with tears, and I turned my head; I didn't want Gray to see weakness. Gray took mercy on me and said, "Hey, I hope things come out OK on Thursday. Now get out of here." I got up and went to the restroom.

When I came back down the hall past Gray's office, I could hear him behind the closed door barking at Ruben. I stopped just short of his office and tried to eavesdrop. Evantie came down the hall toward me so I continued walking towards the back computer room. Later, as I approached my office, I could hear that Ruben and Gray were now in Ruben's and my office. I heard Ruben say with controlled anger, "David, I'm going to ask you for the last time to stop talking to me like this. *I'm* not yelling at *you.*" As I entered the office, Gray grabbed me by the shoulders and asked me to step back outside. Ruben said, "No way, Gray, I want her to witness this." Gray pushed me outside and shut the door. I heard Ruben tell Gray, "I'm not putting up with this, Gray," and Ruben walked out of the office. Gray started to follow Ruben down the hall towards the door, and then he saw me walking towards Ruben. Gray gave up and ducked into his office.

I walked Ruben out and asked him if he was OK. "Did you hear any of that?" he asked. "I heard enough, Ruben. He's just pushing your buttons and trying to get you to blow up. David Gray is doing Evantie's dirty work for him." Ruben responded, "I know, and I didn't buy into it at all. Weren't you proud of me?" "Yes, very. You did a good job of controlling yourself, and he's the one that lost it. He sounded like a maniac." Ruben got into his car and reached out shake my hand. He said, "Hey Dar, don't worry too much about this MRI stuff. There's no way you have MS. You're in too good of shape. It's probably just something stupid like AIDs." We both smiled and laughed.

As I walked back down the hall towards my office, Mattivi pulled me into his office. He told me that Evantie was looking for me because the Acting Commissioner of Customs was about to call for a briefing on the tanker car case. I sat down, closed my eyes and shook my head. This was the last thing I needed. Concerned, Mattivi asked, "Hey, are you all right? You don't look your gorgeous self. What's wrong?" Just then Evantie summoned me into his office. He handed me the phone, and I briefed the Acting Commissioner, Stan Wallace. Wallace sounded nice enough for a politician. He thanked me for the great job I was doing, but he sounded condescending and shallow. Sometimes they can be as shallow as teaspoons.

Chapter Eleven

The Botched Controlled Delivery

The tanker car had been delivered to San Bernardino, was under surveillance, and my warrant had been written. Three days later, I got a call from Ruben. Just the day prior, Evantie had foolishly pulled surveillance from the tanker car assuming that we had given it enough time. I argued his decision to no avail. It had been my experience that crooks would wait weeks before attempting to pick up a large load. This gives them a chance to set up counter-surveillance on the load and see if it's cool or not. They're not stupid; they know how stingy cops will be about footing the bill for a manpower intensive surveillance.

I was at the U.S. Attorney's office with Yvette at the time Ruben called. When he started off with, "Are you sitting down?" I knew something was wrong. Ruben explained how the day after Evantie pulled surveillance off of the controlled delivery tanker car, the crooks popped the top and made entry. "What!" I responded. "How the hell did they do that? That's impossible!" "No, it's not, Dar" Ruben said. "It's the damnedest thing. They jury-rigged a mechanism with a tripod and a pulley and extracted the hatch-port valve system with two forklifts. (The valve system is a system of valves that extend from the opening of the hatch on top of the tanker car to the bottom of the car, used to fill and extract the commodity as well as pressurize or depressurize.) When they hoisted up the valve system and saw that their load was gone, they split. They even left some of their tools there." I couldn't believe what I was hearing. I was furious. I told Yvette, and she and I were both extremely frustrated with the situation. "If Evantie had left the surveillance crew on for just one more day, we would have gotten the off-load crew," I told her. She responded, "I can't believe that they wouldn't keep surveillance on this for just a couple of more days. I've had agencies watch controlled deliveries for weeks." I was embarrassed that my agency had done this and was convinced that their lack of support for my case was because of the grievances filed by Ruben and me. Had Easel the Weasel been the case agent on this case, surveillance on the tanker car would have lasted two or three weeks, and Ruben and I both knew it. I could sense that Yvette was beginning to see a pattern of non-support for me from my agency. Yvette was both smart and objective. She knew that something was very wrong here. As embarrassed as I was, I was also glad that someone else, especially a federal prosecutor, was seeing what my agency was capable of with their own two eyes. I recognized how important it was that she begin to see what was going on here, but I wouldn't know until later just how important.

Ruben, Renado and I spent the rest of the week running down leads, fighting with the FBI and meeting with Yvette.

Darlene with Task Force Officers during controlled delivery cross-country

Chapter Twelve

Internal Affairs

On the evening of April 14, 1998, I got a call at home from Evantie. "Some lady from San Francisco will be coming to the office tomorrow to talk to you about your EEO case," he informed me. I reminded him that I had approved sick leave for a doctor's appointment on Thursday afternoon. He told me that if I came in the morning, I would still make it in plenty of time for my testing. I complied, thinking that maybe someone was finally going to take this EEO stuff seriously and investigate it. I could not sleep that night. I was too worried about what the MRI might bring. Ben tried to comfort me, but I could see the worry on his face.

The next morning, April 15, 1998, I went to the office. It wasn't long before Evantie called me into his office via the intercom. He introduced me to Lana Janston, Group Supervisor from San Francisco. Evantie left the office closing the door behind him. As he was leaving, he had an evil smirk on his face, and I knew there was something fishy going on. Ms. Janston informed me that I was under investigation for wrongful release of information. As she began reading me my rights I interrupted her and told her that Evantie had conveyed to me that she was here to talk to me about my EEO complaint. Janston replied that the investigation did involve my EEO complaint. I then told her that I refused to talk to her until I spoke to my attorney. She ordered me to sign the rights warnings, but I told her I had approved sick leave today and walked out of the office. I went to my desk and sent an emergency page to my attorney. Ruben was sitting there and asked what was going on. As I briefed him, the phone rang. It was my attorney. I explained to him what had happened, and he asked to speak to Ms. Janston.

Ruben was irate. "What a cruel thing to do, knowing about your medical test today. Hang in there Dar. Don't let them get to you." After a few minutes, Ms. Janston came over the intercom telling me to pick up line three. It was my attorney. "It's a witch hunt," he said, "they are saying that you wrongfully released information contained in your EEO report. Look, they are violating your Title 7 rights and Privacy Act rights, but you have to participate in this grilling or they can fire you. Now, go to your doctor's appointment and afterwards you and I will talk more about strategy before you go in there, OK?" I agreed and left for my appointment.

My husband Ben surprised me by showing up at the clinic. I was so glad to see him. I told him about Evantie deceptively calling me into this meeting. Ben said, "That Evantie, he's a real piece of work." Ben stayed with me during my entire test to comfort me. They told me it would be a week or so before I got the results of my test back.

I talked strategy with my attorney and went back to the office where I signed the rights warning and answered Ms. Janston's stupid questions. She told me that this was about the letters of commendation that I had included in my EEO complaint. These letters of commendation were from prosecutors and DEA supervisors commending me on my work. I didn't even write these letters; they did. In the content of these letters they put in several case numbers and names of bad guys. I included these letters in my complaint to demonstrate that I was an outstanding agent. Just then it hit me; there were very similar "hero" letters hanging up and down the walls of this office. I showed Janston the photos and reminded her that the office has a cleaning team, as well as other non-agency personnel, who routinely enter the office and view these photos. She just smirked at me.

The questions that Ms. Janston had were all designed to elicit a "yes" or "no" answer. If I had followed her instructions to answer with a mere "yes" or "no" with no explanation on my part, the statement would have appeared very damning to me. So I refused to answer as she wished and insisted on writing out explanations. She reminded me several times that she had a plane to catch and that she did not intend for this interview to last this long. I cursed her under my breath and took my time, doing the best job that I could under the stressful circumstances. It took me five hours to complete my statement. Ms. Janston missed her plane.

The timing of this investigation was brilliant on their part. The promotion list for GS 13 had just been released, and I was in the top 10. There were 11 openings, and I was assured to get a promotion. The only way that they could promote someone over me was if I had a red file (an active open Internal Affairs investigation). By policy, no one can be promoted with a red file. They couldn't find anything legitimate to get me on, so they just made up lies. They knew it would not hold up, but that wasn't the purpose. They had accomplished their mission, and I was taken off the list. That night, I went to the gym before going home. I swam until I could barely pull myself out of the pool. All I could see was Evantie's arrogant smirk as he called me into his office and Janston began reading me my rights. As I fell asleep that night, I began having the dream again, but something woke me up, and I couldn't get back to sleep.

The next day Ruben, Jerry, Renado, Mattivi, Gray, and I hit a business in San Bernardino, as well as several other houses connected to the tanker car seizure. Two days later, after endless interviews and running down leads, I arrested a key player in the infamous Arellano-Felix Narcotics Organization. I flipped him (term used for getting defendants to cooperate), and Yvette and I put him in protective custody and began interviewing the CI (Confidential Informant). Yvette and I had lunch together, and she asked me why I wasn't getting any help on my case. I had authored, presented and achieved OCDETF (Organized Crime Drug Enforcement Task Force) status for this case and for the rail project. This meant that I was supposed to be supplied with a full task force to handle the investigation and project. Evantie and SAIC Brinkley had pulled all of my support. I laughed sarcastically when I told her, "You're looking at the OCDETF task force of me, myself, and I!" I trusted Yvette and told her what was going on. She looked at me and said, "They can't do that; that's undermining a criminal case in order to shut you up." I shook my head. Yvette replied in a very disturbed voice, "You know, there's a term for this—obstruction of justice."

The day after my working lunch with Yvette, April 19, 1998, I had my follow-up doctor's appointment. I was very relieved to hear that I did not have MS. The doctor did, however, tell me that Epstein Bar Syndrome, commonly referred to as Mono, caused the ringing in my ears and several other symptoms. He said I had probably picked it up from the pool I had been swimming in. He added that because the virus had gone undiagnosed for so long with an extended low-grade fever, the ringing in my ears would probably be permanent. My blood pressure was also extremely low, and my white blood cell count was very high. He told me that my body fat content was so low that it was messing up my menstrual cycle and causing a hormonal imbalance. Extended exhaustion, continued lack of deep REM sleep and too much stress were taking their toll. But other than that, I was just fine. He looked at me and asked what was going on in my life that was causing all of this. I just smiled, looked down at the ground and shook my head and laughed. He said, "I'm glad you find all this amusing, but you won't find it so funny when you're in the morgue, Agent Catalan." He gave me several prescriptions and told me that I had better slow down and get some rest.

That night the dream came, and I was back at Fort Huachuca, Arizona, my last assignment as a Captain on active duty with the Military Police Corps. I was in my old office sitting in my chair. I could almost smell the pungent aroma of the old wood. It felt comfortable to be back there, like seeing an old friend again. I loved the Army and always felt in control there. Things were simpler then.

The little toddler appeared in the hallway in front of me. He was filthy and crying and began walking away. He looked back at me and called me with his beautiful, deep blue eyes to follow him down the dark stairs. We walked into what used to be the old morgue area. He turned to me and smiled, causing a strange sensation of peacefulness to come over me. As I began slowly walking towards him, I noticed that I had my military dress blues on. I took his delicate, little, dirty hand in my white glove and then was startled awake by my alarm. I ran into the bathroom and threw up.

Chapter Thirteen

Routine Business

On April 22, 1998, our office had to serve a search warrant in East L.A. We were to meet in the parking lot at Costello Park by the pool. As I sat there waiting for the other agents to show up, I thought about the name of this place. Lou Costello, of the famous "Abbott and Costello," had built the park in honor of his son. Costello's son had evidently drowned, and Lou Costello wanted kids to have the opportunity to learn how to swim so that more drownings might be prevented. I thought of how painful it must have been to have lost a child. It broke my heart. I knew that I would just die if I lost one of my kids, which is why the dream worried me so much. I was afraid that it was some sort of warning. A part of me wished that I could quit my job and stay home with my kids so that I always knew they were all right. Instead, I pulled out my laptop and worked on my EEO retaliation while I waited for the guys.

We briefed in the parking lot, suited up and waited for the tow truck. The house that we were going to hit had a cast iron security gate on the door and iron bars on the windows. The plan was to hook the tow truck's hook and wench onto the front door and have the tow truck pull the door off after we gave "knock notice," a legal requirement to announce warrant entry before actual entry is made. When we arrived at the house, I grabbed the hook and ran toward the door. As I approached the porch, I knew that this was a bad idea. The house was old and had a rickety porch with brick pillars holding up the roof. I hooked the door and ran off the porch. Jerry Johnston and a uniformed

LAPD officer yelled, "Federal Agents with a search warrant, open the door." Just then the tow truck floored it, and the door went flying through the air and crashed into the brick pillars. Just as the brick pillar collapsed and the porch roof started to cave in, I noticed that there was an old black man standing in the doorway with his hand where the door knob used to be. This poor man was in shock.

Our tow truck pulley was probably one of the most hilarious things I had ever seen. As we were running up to the house to make entry, everyone was laughing so hard we could barely make it through the door. As we secured the house and completed the search, we all walked outside to look at the porch. We stood there laughing. If I hadn't seen it with my own two eyes, I'd never have believed it. Just then, I noticed the old black man with two officers, sitting in a chair on his front yard. He was crying and looking up at the damage to his home. His son was the one whom the warrant was directed towards, yet he was the one who received the damage. All of a sudden I stopped laughing; it wasn't funny anymore. I felt a tremendous amount of guilt and sorrow for what we had done to this poor old man. I thought about my aging father and how he'd feel if the home that he had worked so hard on for many years had been damaged by a bunch of arrogant federal agents.

I went back to the office and attempted to finish my EEO complaint. Unable to put the poor old man out of my mind, I found it very hard to concentrate. I was angry with myself that I hadn't tried to console him. I felt guilty for having laughed about the visual comedy of the situation. Somehow, I finished the complaint and faxed it to the EEO office. This was a complaint of retaliation based upon the foolish IA investigation regarding letters of commendation I had submitted in my original EEO complaint. My complaint was subsequently dismissed by the Regional Complaint Center on June 26, 1998, with no informal or formal investigation (i.e. none of my witnesses nor I were ever contacted by an EEO counselor on these specific issues). I filed a response to this dismissal on

July 1, 1998, addressing the lack of investigation. Not surprisingly, I never received a response to my complaint or my letter.

On May 22, 1998, I read the article in the *San Diego Union-Tribune* dated May 16, 1998, regarding the lawsuit between Ricardo Sandoval and the U.S. Customs Service. Ervin Rios sent Ruben and me a copy. Ricardo had recently completed a lawsuit against Customs winning $200,000 plus $500,000 in attorney's fees and back pay for discrimination. Sandoval used the same attorneys that Ruben, Sandy, Ervin Rios and I initially used. On the last page of the article I took particular notice of the fact that Sandoval had filed a second lawsuit charging that after he uncovered the existence of a racist ring, he was subjected to a series of internal investigations and falsely accused of crimes.

When I read this I had very mixed emotions. I was consoled that someone who had experienced treatment similar to what I was receiving from my agency had won against Customs. But I also became very worried. If they would come after someone like him (already a GS-13 and a SA for the Office of Internal Affairs) then I'm doomed. I feared that it would be only a matter of time before this all blew up in my face. I also feared that because this agency had lost so badly on the Sandoval Case, Customs would be out for blood, and it could easily be mine.

I called Sandy and read her the article. I told her that I found it very apropos for Customs to use a lawyer from the U.S. Attorney's office and not from our own regional council. To me that was a big indication as to the confidence, or lack thereof, our agency had in its own Regional Council. I remember thinking, "Who knows, maybe Sandy's right. Maybe Customs will be more leery about coming after us now that they have lost the Sandoval lawsuit." You would think that this agency would learn its lesson, but I feared not.

There was a quote in the article from one of the jurors in this case that I found most haunting. Juror Cannon stated that, "Discrimination inside the government is no worse or more widespread that in corporate America," but he added, "The government has a lot more power, and that's when it becomes dangerous." If the general public only knew the power and control that management in this agency possesses over its employees and how they flaunt it, the general public would be disgusted. If my agency felt that we were a threat, they would most certainly put their IA dogs on us.

On June 25, 1998, I was investigated for the second time by my agency for wrongful use of Government Identification. Evidently, someone anonymously called into the IA office and accused me of using my reserve Army identification to gain access to military flights at a reduced or free rate. I was required to commute three hours, one way, from my home to the IA office in Long Beach, California for the second part of this witch-hunt. When I got there, IA Agent Terry Clay escorted me into an interview room. As I sat there having my rights read to me again, I realized just what it was like to be facing a large glass mirror knowing there were people watching me on the other side, the same position that I had put witnesses and defendants in too many times to count. The world looks a lot different when you're sitting on the other side of that table and someone is firing the questions at you. I felt my stomach burn and my anger rise up to my face.

I explained to the IA "rocket scientist" that "the use of one's military I.D. for this purpose was common practice within the Army; it's commonly referred to as 'catching a hop' or 'space available,' and it is not a violation of any policy, and I never did this anyway. Additionally, if it were a violation of policy, that policy would be under the jurisdiction of U.S. Army Criminal Investigation Division (CID), not U.S. Customs Service. So basically, Terry, all of this was done without you having the sense to check if my alleged offense was even a violation." I grabbed the written version of the rights they had read to me and made me sign, pointed at it, and said, "I want a copy of this. This bull— is over." At first Terry refused to give me a copy, but after a verbal altercation, I left with a copy. This would be the only evidence I had that I had ever been there for this amazing blunder.

That evening I went to the gym and ran five miles. With every step I took, I felt as though I was going to explode. My chest was tight. I knew that, once again, this IA witch-hunt had conveniently occurred when I had made the BQL for promotion to GS-13, giving me a red file and eliminating me from the BQL. This was a cheap but clever shot designed to pressure me not to testify on Ruben's upcoming deposition for his federal lawsuit against Customs, and to teach me a lesson. I felt like a helpless child being bullied by the neighborhood thug.

That night I had the dream again. I was standing in my bedroom and the beautiful toddler appeared before me. He was filthy and had tears in his eyes. I picked him up and took him to the sink in my bedroom and sat him down. I took a washcloth and tried to clean his little hands. He looked at me with his angelic eyes, took my hand and smiled. The next thing I knew, I was standing in a beautiful pasture holding him. The grass was technicolor green and waved in the wind. There were cattle grazing all around. I put the toddler down and he took my hand, motioning for me to come with him.

We walked up to the top of a small hill overlooking a pleasant valley. There was a beautiful old farmhouse that someone was adding on to. Not too far from the house was a corral. There were cattle chutes where cows are steered into, in order to inoculate them. Between the flat fence posts, I could see the back of a young man working the cows. I attempted to move closer, but for some reason I could not. From what I could tell, the man was in his early to mid 30's. He was just under six feet and a little stocky, but not fat. He had short brown hair and though he was wearing a flannel shirt, blue jeans and boots, he had an angelic and almost spiritual aura about him. I could hear his deep raspy voice as he coaxed the cows. He spoke with a British or Australian accent; I was unable to distinguish which it was. Although he sounded a lot like Mel Gibson, somehow I knew he wasn't. I then noticed that he had two dogs working with him. One of the dogs was nipping at the heels of the cows. The man yelled at the dog, calling it "mate."

Then I noticed something very strange. Off at a distance I could see what appeared to be a kangaroo hopping around. I also saw a pond nearby with ducks. Everything was so beautiful and peaceful. The man's voice, though deep and at times gritty, seemed very comforting and almost familiar. Yet somehow, I knew he was a stranger. I noticed that he had an old flatbed truck with two packs of cigarettes lying on the hood. One was wadded up and the other had just been opened. There were beautifully colored wildflowers sprinkled throughout the grass. I wanted so badly to stay there and walk over to see who this stranger was. Then I felt the toddler squeezing my hand, and I knew it was time to go. I took one last look and attempted to see the man's face. I kept hoping that he would turn our way and see us there, but he didn't.

The next morning when I awoke, I lay there wondering what all of this meant. Those few short moments in my dream were the most peaceful ones I had had in years. I began wondering where this place could have been. I remembered the kangaroo and the accent of the man and wondered if it was Australia, but that couldn't be right. From what I knew about Australia, it was pretty dry, brown and rocky, kind of like west Texas. Why did the toddler take me there, and why wasn't I allowed to see the face of the man? Did these dreams have any meaning, or was I just cracking under pressure? And the location—why in the world was I in Australia or England? Why not my beautiful home in the Appalachian mountains of Kentucky? None of this made sense.

Then I thought of something I heard a LAPD narcotics officer say to me once. In LAPD they were only allowed to work major narcotics for three years for fear of burn out. I had been working major narcotics investigations for 11 years. I was convinced that I was losing my mind. I wanted so badly to tell Ben, Ruben or maybe even Sandy about these dreams, but I had this sense that I was supposed to keep this a secret, like I would be breaking confidence if I told them. I was also afraid that they would lock me in a rubber room.

The next day, I filed an EEO complaint of retaliation regarding the second part of this witch-hunt. EEO Supervisor Conales never assigned me an investigator for this issue. I was confident she received the complaint because I faxed it and sent it certified mail. I had both the fax transmittal and the certified mail confirmation to prove she received the complaint. I followed up with her by leaving her a voicemail. She was blatantly ignoring my complaints.

On June 25, 1998, SA Edwin Easel was promoted to GS-13, despite the fact that he had a lower CAAPS score than I did. Had Winkowsky followed policy, he would have reported Easel for the incident in which he had taken heroin home, and Easel would have received the mandatory 90 days on the bricks, or even firing, eliminating him from this promotion. When Ruben and I confirmed this news, we both felt ill. We left the office early that day in preparation for the "dumpster diving" I had to do that night. We knew that this would give us an opportunity to talk.

I went home and tried to get some sleep, but I just tossed and turned. I was so angry that they had promoted Easel the Weasel over Ruben and me. He had much less time in Customs than we did, not to mention no prior law enforcement experience and the inability to make a case on his own without being spoon-fed. My stomach burned, and I gave up trying to sleep. The phone rang and it was Sandy. She said, "I heard the news. That is so absurd! You and Ruben run circles around that weasel, and everyone knows it. If this isn't blatant retaliation I don't know what is." She spent most of the conversation trying to console me. Sandy's the best girlfriend I had ever had. She was the most honest person I'd ever met, not to mention, the most loyal friend. I needed this phone call; it lifted my spirits.

I readied for my trash run. This was for a fraud case on a businessman in Temecula, California. The crook had completed a "Corporate Bleed-Out" of his business and had put the screws to all the other partners and employees. He had also filed a phony bankruptcy. He had made quite a bit of money through the business that he was bankrupting, thus having the need to launder this money through other front companies overseas. When he wired the money back and forth, he committed several Customs violations, including money laundering. I was going that night to his business to dig in his trash dumpster, hence the slang "dumpster diving," for documents or other evidence. It's surprising the things that stupid crooks throw in their trash.

When I got there at about midnight, Ruben and Jerry Johnston were already there. I was on time, but they still gave me a hard time about making them wait. Like me, neither one of them had been able to sleep. We were all tired and grouchy. They set up their surveillance on me in the adjacent parking lot. I snuck over to the dumpsters, and as I approached the back of the crook's business, I smelled something horrible. It smelled like a skunk. I looked around and couldn't see anything, so I jumped into the dumpster. Just then I heard and felt a loud thud at the bottom of the dumpster. Out ran a very large skunk. I ducked down in the dumpster, held my breath, and squinted my eyes shut. Then I heard laughter off at a distance. Ruben and Jerry burst out laughing, and I couldn't help but laugh with them. Although I was lucky that the skunk hadn't sprayed me directly, I still smelled of trash and skunk.

I found some great documents and other evidence and returned to the parking lot where Jerry and Ruben were still laughing at me. I had parked my car a distance away and needed a lift. Jerry said, "Hop in the back of my truck here, woman. You sure as hell aren't riding in my cab." I looked at Ruben. He was still laughing at me. "Don't look at me! You stink; you're not riding in my car." Using some colorful language, I told them to forget it and walked to my car. They followed me to my car making stinky jokes the whole way and having a great time at my expense. I didn't care. I was just happy to have gotten what I needed to nail the crook for fraud and money laundering. It had all been worth it. The next day I briefed my AUSA for fraud, Jim McNarra, on this case and he was very pleased.

Chapter Fourteen

Disciplinary Action

On July 30, 1998, EEO Supervisor Conales lied in a statement regarding the reason for the removal of my EEO counselor Anna Francisco. She claimed that she had spoken with Francisco on numerous occasions about following the time requirements, insinuating that Anna was somehow being negligent in her duties. Conales said it was her intention to remove her as early as October 1997. I called Anna and read the statement to her. She was appalled. Anna told me that Conales never mentioned any of this to her. Anna just confirmed what I already knew. Conales was a snake.

On August 3, 1998, I was in my office typing up reports on the computer when Evantie came in and said, "Hey, Dar, can you come see me please?" I thought, "Oh great! What the heck is this all about?" Ruben wasn't there, and I was hesitant to walk into Evantie's office without a witness, but I did anyway. "Why don't you shut the door?" he said. I responded very respectfully, "I'd rather not, sir." Evantie smirked and shook his head in disgust and said "OK." He handed me a letter of disciplinary action for wrongful release of information based upon the letters of commendation I had given to Anna in my EEO complaint. This meeting with Evantie was, coincidentally, just a few weeks before I was scheduled to testify in Ruben's federal lawsuit.

I glanced over the letter and knew it was imperative that I control my temper. I very sarcastically said to Evantie, "Is that it?" He responded, "Well, don't you have any questions or anything?" I told him I didn't and turned to walk away. He stopped me and said, "Well, you have to sign here that you received the letter." I walked to his desk, grabbed the pen from his fancy pen holder, signed the document and started to leave again. "Hey, Dar, wait a minute. How's that fraud case coming along?" I told him how positive the prosecutor was and that we were confident that based upon what was seized in prior warrants and in my trash runs, we would most certainly be able to get this guy on fraud and money laundering charges. Evantie began asking questions in a very negative way. It was clear that he was trying to undermine my case. I got frustrated with his subversive line of questioning and told him, "Hey, if you don't like what were doing on the case, go talk to the prosecutor yourself." He responded with, "Well, I may just do that. You've been on this thing way too long, and I obviously need to move this guy along and get this thing wrapped up." "You do that Evantie. You do that."

I went back to my desk and read the letter. I took particular note that on the last page there was a paragraph that could be considered extremely coercive. The paragraph read, "A copy of this letter will be placed in your Official Personnel Folder (OPF) for a period not to exceed three (3) years from the date of the letter. The letter may be removed by local management, with my concurrence, should circumstances warrant such action." I thought to myself, "Gee, I wonder what these circumstances would be? Drop your EEO complaint and refuse to testify for Ruben?" Had I done this, I'm sure that all would have been well. It was signed by Dirk Kirkland of the disciplinary review board. Everyone in Customs knew that Kirkland was one of Brinkley's cronies. Now he had empowered local management, the very same people whom we had filed complaints about, to be in a position to magically make this letter disappear if I "played ball."

Ruben walked in and saw me fuming. "What's going on Dar? What's the matter?" I tossed the letter over to him. He began reading it, stopped, came over to my desk, grabbed me and hustled me and the letter out to his car. We went for a ride, and I read him the whole letter and told him how Evantie was now planning to undermine my fraud case. I reminded him that the average fraud case, unlike dope cases, usually takes about three years to develop, and I had only worked on this one for a little over a year. He told me not to worry; it was just another scare tactic to get me to blow up. He reminded me of how absurd this was. Just because they couldn't find anything else on me they had to come up with something. That night I went to the gym again and swam until I almost drowned. I lost count of laps and time. I paid for it the next day.

On August 5, 1998, Evantie and I met with my federal prosecutor, McNarra, on my fraud case. I had met with him numerous times already, and he was extremely pleased with my work and the progress on the case. Given the enthusiastic support of the prosecutor, it would be interesting to see just how Evantie would try to torpedo this case. The prosecutor briefed Evantie on our progress and our intentions with the case. I wouldn't have believed it if I hadn't seen it and heard it with my own two eyes and ears. Evantie actually had the nerve to try to undermine me before the prosecutor. He made multiple comments that were clearly meant to make me look bad, but my prosecutor, much to Evantie's dismay, was defending me. As the meeting went on, AUSA McNarra was looking at me very suspiciously as if to say, "What's going on here?"

When the meeting was over, Evantie left and I stayed behind to brief McNarra. As soon as I shut his door for privacy he said, "What the heck's going on here, Dar?" "This is what happens in our agency when you are not part of the 'good old boy' system," I replied. McNarra looked at me with pity and shook his head. I was embarrassed but really didn't want to get into the whole ordeal with him; so I didn't. I just assured him that I'd take care of everything and things would be OK. I was just happy that Evantie wasn't successful in his efforts to ruin my case with my prosecutor. I was pleased that this AUSA saw right through his tactics. I reminded myself that against a federal prosecutor, Evantie was about as bright as a burnt out light bulb.

That night I was desperately hoping that my toddler would come and take me back to the farm. I tossed and turned all night. I felt ill, and I couldn't sleep. The toddler never came.

On August 7, 1998, at approximately 1400hrs, I checked my Customs inbox. I found photocopies of reports of investigation (ROI) of closed cases. There were notes on these ROI's from our new Acting Group Supervisor, Dudley O'Shea, asking me to modify or explain them. Dudley O'Shea was another of Brinkley's well-known cronies. O'Shea's wife was the SAIC/LA in the Internal Affairs Office. Other supervisors who had previously approved these ROI's displayed no concerns about them when they were approved. I have never, in my almost 11 years of service in the agency, observed agents being asked to modify reports on closed cases; and even if I wanted to modify them, our computer system will not allow you to modify ROI's once approved.

Additionally, I canvassed the RAIC/Riverside office, and no other agents were being required to complete this type of task on closed cases. I asked Bob Mattivi, the old salt of the office with almost 30 years of experience and smartest guy in the office, if he had ever observed anything like this. Bob shook his head in disbelief and said, "Boy, Darlene, O'Shea's only been on the job a couple of days, and he's already going after you." He had never seen anything like this. Mattivi knew more about criminal investigations than guys like O'Shea would ever know. I trusted Bob and knew that he was right on the money.

On August 11, 1998, I observed SSA Terry Clay, "Mr. IA," walking down the hall. I took particular note of the fact that he was walking right past all of the "hero" photos hanging on the walls, which had a heck of a lot more information in them than the ones I was investigated for. As I passed him, I looked at one of the photos, causing him to look also. I looked back at him and shook my head. He got my point, looked embarrassed and kept walking. As I walked to my office, I realized that the new GS-13 list had just come out, and I had once again made the BQL. I felt worn down and hopeless. I knew that I was about to be investigated again on some phony charge, once more tagging me with a red file and tossing me off the list. I went home in disgust.

On August 17, 1998, I filed a response to my letter of disciplinary action. Shortly thereafter, I received a response from Kirkland. His response was as follows: "You expressed very strong concerns in your grievance letter that the letter of reprimand contained language you found coercive in nature. Please be advised that the language in the reprimand states that if you should separate from the Service before this letter is removed from your OPF, it will be removed and destroyed in accordance with applicable regulation." I thought to myself, "How clever for Mr. Kirkland to change the actual wording of this letter and conveniently leave out the part about 'if circumstances warrant local management may remove this letter.'" I read the letter to Ruben and said, "What a moron!"

I called Sandy that night, as I did most every night. My husband thought that we chattered about this stuff too much and got each other in an uproar. I don't know, maybe he's right. Still, Sandy and I did a good job of motivating each other to fight back. Sandy is one brave woman, and I have a lot of respect for her opinion, not to mention that I sometimes need to hear a woman's point of view. I'm in a male dominated field, surrounded by men all day, and all that testosterone can start to have an effect on a person. Sandy cheered me up, as she always does, and I was grateful for it.

September 3, 1998, I went to the U.S. Attorney's office for a meeting with AUSA Yvette. Afterwards, I spoke with Arnold Connez. He informed me that in the last two staff meetings, SAIC Brinkley got up in front of all the supervisors and trashed the EEO process and those who were filing EEO complaints. He also told me that Brinkley had mentioned Sandy and me by name, stating that we were troublemakers and that I was a hothead.

That night when I got home, Sandy, Shannon Getz, a former FBI agent and fellow whistleblower, and I had a phone conversation.

Shannon told us that another supervisor, Ron James, had told her the same thing. Ron James was my first supervisor in Customs and also one of the nicest men I had ever met. However, he was also spineless, and I knew I could not count on him to testify to what he had heard. I reminded myself that not all Customs managers were evil; there were those who were evil but had a spine, then there were those who were evil and had no spine and there were also those who were not evil but had no spine. James fit well into this last category. We decided to file a Class Action EEO complaint, and when we later pitched this idea to Ruben, Ervin Rios, Ricardo Sandoval and Arnold Connez, they agreed to join us. I was elected to write the complaint, and I stayed up until midnight that night writing. Sandy did her usual excellent editing job, and we submitted it.

Chapter Fifteen

Threat Via Mail

On September 9, 1998, I woke up hoping that all this stuff was just some sort of bizarre dream. When I got home from work that day I checked the mail. I took it into the house along with the other mail and began sorting through it. I opened the bills first, may as well get the bad news out of the way, and then threw away the junk mail. My kids were all trying to talk to me at once the way kids do when you first come home from work. They required my complete attention, and thus, I was only half paying attention to what was there.

With all of my training and experience in terrorism and letter bombs, you would think I would have noticed that this letter didn't have a return address on the outside, but I didn't. As I was listening to my kids chatter, I opened the innocent looking "invitation." At first, I only noticed that it was ripped and folded like a child folds notes. I assumed it was just a note or invitation for one of my kids. As I responded to my kids, I smoothed out the wrinkles of the letter and wondered why it was ripped. Then I read the words, "SHUT UP AND RESIGN OR YOUR FLETC PICTURES WILL BE MAILED TO THE TABLOIDS AND YOUR FAMILY WILL BE HUMILIATED."

A familiar feeling came over me. My body felt weak, and I recognized this feeling from an incident that happened when I was younger. I was about eight years old when I saw my neighbor shoot another neighbor right in front of me. I still remember being in shock at what I saw. I watched my neighbor, Vernon Steller, being threatened by this huge guy we all called "Crazy Dave." I could see the fear and anger on Mr. Steller's face. I knew something awful was about to happen. As Mr. Steller watched Crazy Dave Jackson storm away to his house, the anguish and fear grew on the smaller man's face. Mr. Steller then ran into his own home. His little boy, Ryan, was running behind him pulling on his clothes begging him, "Don't Dad, don't, please don't," as if he already knew what was about to happen. I watched with curiosity, wondering what this little boy knew that I didn't.

Mr. Steller came out of the house with his son Ryan hanging on his arm, still begging him to stop. Mr. Steller had a gun, and I felt numb. I had been riding my bike and stopped to observe this argument, and now I was frozen, unable to move. My mind was racing in fear for little Ryan. I wanted to grab him away from this and run with him to my house, but I couldn't move. Mr. Steller began yelling, "Come on outside; now's the time, now's the time!" Finally, someone appeared at the door, only it wasn't Crazy Dave. It was his brother-in-law, Mr. Witherspout. Mr. Witherspout seemed not to be so mad and crazy, and I thought he was coming out to diffuse the situation. I felt a short-lived sense of relief. Mr. Witherspout always seemed to be a nice, calm, practical kind of guy, and I thought he'd be able to reason with Mr. Steller.

The two men met in front of the large tree that looked like a Christmas tree standing between their two houses. How queer it seemed that this took place in front of the very tree that these two neighbors argued so much about. I never understood why Mr. Steller hated that tree so much; I always thought it was a beautiful tree, particularly in the winter when decorated for Christmas. I know now that their hatred had nothing to do with this tree.

The men were talking, and little Ryan was still begging his dad to go back into the house. Because they were talking and not shouting, I thought that everything would be all right. Then I heard a pop, and Mr. Witherspout fell to the ground moaning. Poor little Ryan started screaming and crying and pulling his dad back into the house. I looked into Mr. Steller's eyes. They looked dead and numb just like I was feeling. Suddenly, a rush of energy came to me and I flew away on my bike and ran up the steps into my home. Nothing around me made sense, and as I tried to tell my parents what had just happened, I couldn't get my words to make sense either. It was like I was dreaming. Nothing seemed real. The air had a strange smell, reminding me of the time I got shocked plugging in something and could smell the electricity running through my body.

I had long since forgotten that feeling. When I read this letter, I was there again. Nothing made sense around me, and the air smelled of electricity. I stood there frozen as my kids were talking to me. I wasn't hearing them. Suddenly my daughter, Rochelle, grabbed the letter and said, "Is this for me?" I grabbed the letter back and tried not to let my kids see my reaction for fear of alarming them. "No, this is for me," I said.

I went upstairs and tried to dial a phone number. It took me many times to correctly page my husband. My fingers kept hitting the wrong numbers as though I had no control over them. Finally, I heard my husband's voicemail, and I felt a sense of relief as I paged him to our home. The FLETC pictures this note was referring to were the pictures that were taken by my ex-boyfriend 10 years ago. We went through the Federal Law Enforcement Training Center (FLETC) together in Glynco, Georgia. This is the Department of Treasury's training academy for most of its federal employees, including federal agents. While at FLETC, I did a very stupid thing; hindsight is 20/20. I allowed my ex-boyfriend, a Customs employee, to take very explicit, embarrassing, nude photos of me, a mistake I'll regret for the rest of my life. When I broke off the relationship, my ex-boyfriend was so angry that the day after he went to work and showed my pictures, and those of several other women, to a few Customs pilots and Air Interdiction Officers (AIOs) making very derogatory remarks about us.

The pilots and AIOs all knew me, and several of them took offense that he was doing this. One of them contacted Customs Internal Affairs, and my ex-boyfriend was investigated. The IA investigator, Donna Jones, interviewed me and told me what my ex-boyfriend had done. She also informed me that she had seized the photos and that they would be destroyed upon conclusion of the investigation. My ex-boyfriend was forced to resign and now works for another agency.

As I continued staring at this note, I looked inside the envelope as though if I kept looking, an explanation of what was going on might magically appear. Then the phone rang. It was my husband. I told him about the letter and he was not at all surprised. He comforted me and assured me that it was just a bluff to scare me. My husband is the wisest man I know, and even though I realized he was probably right, I was still in disbelief. The air still smelled like electricity, and my body felt weak. I suddenly remembered that I was putting fingerprints all over the letter and probably destroying any evidence that we would need to catch whoever did this. Once again, in my shock, all of my training and experience had gone right out the window. I put the letter in a clear plastic bag.

I called Sandy and told her what had just happened. The anger in her voice was so strong that it overpowered the numbness I was feeling. She paged our attorney, and we had a conference call. Our attorney's reaction was very similar to my husband's, one of, "This doesn't surprise me. This agency is capable of anything; we've seen this behavior before." My attorney then said something that snapped me right out of my shock. He told me that my agency, in order to defend themselves, would accuse me of sending this letter to myself in order to boost my lawsuit. How inflammatory! I couldn't believe this! This seemed the most ridiculous concept imaginable; as if I would embarrass my kids and my family to boost a lawsuit, which was at this point a slam-dunk anyway. As absurd as this sounded, I knew he was right. I knew that was exactly the type of lame tactic my agency would attempt. I told him that it wouldn't work because I would just pass a polygraph. He reminded me that polygraphs are not accepted in Federal Civil Court. I was so frustrated!

Sandy and I contacted Ervin. We now had three enraged people on the phone, but I was the only one who expressed any shock at the situation. Ervin and Sandy were very supportive and tried to console me. One positive thing about situations such as these is that it certainly weeds out the fair-weather friends. Sandy, Ervin, and Ruben Sandoval are rare, true-blue friends who understand the meaning of loyalty. After my conversation with Sandy and Ervin, I called Ruben. He, like I, was in complete shock. He asked me if it would be alright for him to talk to a U.S. Attorney he knew and trusted and elicit advice from her. I agreed.

That night I couldn't sleep. Again, I wanted so badly for the toddler to take me to the beautiful farm and see the strange man there. But the toddler never came.

September 10, 1998, I had to get up, go to work, and act as though nothing had happened just in case someone in my office was watching me for a reaction. I took half the day off in order to meet with Ruben and Sandy at the U.S. Attorney's office. We had previously agreed, before I ever received the note, to meet at the U.S. Attorney's office to sign a Class EEO complaint that all of us, (Sandy Nunn, Ruben Sandoval, Arnold Connez, Shannon Getz, Ervin Rios, Ricardo Sandoval and myself) had agreed to file. Before I left the office, I got a call from Ervin. He told me that he had been so frustrated that he had gone and talked to the editor of the *L.A. Times*. I couldn't believe he had done this! I was angry and scolded him for his indiscretion. I told him that he should have talked to me first because I was taking this to the U.S. Marshals to pursue this criminally, and the media would most certainly get in the way. Ervin apologized in a tone of voice that made me feel like I had just kicked a puppy. I knew he meant well, and I felt bad for scolding him. Ervin was a very honest and big-hearted guy. He had been there for me so many times, and I knew he was just trying to do something that would make us not feel so helpless.

I met with Ruben and Sandy at the AUSA's office. Ruben told me that he talked to his friend, AUSA Penny Salvador. She told him that I should put the letter in a secure place like a safety deposit box or a safe. She also agreed that I should contact the Postal Inspectors but not give the original to them unless they guaranteed that my agency would in no way be involved in the investigation. Ruben offered to make copies and keep the original for me in his safety deposit box. I agreed; I trusted Ruben with my life. We had been partners in the field for many years now and had backed each other up in many tight situations. We never dreamed that we would have to depend on each other so heavily in this type of situation.

I was running late for my meeting with our attorney, and my stress level was over the breaking point. I was on the I-10 freeway when my pager went off. It was my husband's pager number with a 911 suffix. With everything that was happening, I immediately thought the worst. I got off of the freeway in a bad part of L.A. and began to panic. I couldn't find a pay phone anywhere, and when I did, it was broken. Finally, I found a pay phone that worked and called my husband's voicemail. I left a message telling him to leave me a number on my pager where I could call him, because I was calling from a pay phone that didn't accept incoming calls. As I was waiting, I began to notice where I was. This was the area I had been in during the L.A. riots. I saw that the old, dilapidated buildings which had burned down had been replaced by new ones, but it was still a hell-hole. In my nervousness I began to laugh. My laughter soon turned to tears. I began sobbing. I was sure something awful had happened. I then saw a marked unit. I flagged him down, and sure enough, he had a cell phone. I called my husband again and paged him to the cell phone.

While we were waiting, the officer began asking me about Customs and indicated that he was interested in becoming an agent. I was tying his unit up so I felt obligated to give him information about our agency and how to apply. Ironically, I had been the office recruiter for Customs. I took his business card and told him I would send him the applications he needed to apply. I knew I would never send them. No one should be recruited into this agency, no one. My husband never called, so I proceeded to our attorney's office. Upon my arrival to the attorney's office, my pager went off. It was my husband calling me from home. I immediately jumped on the phone in the lobby and called home. My husband told me that the 911 page was because I had screwed up the kid's bus passes. This was not my idea of what a 911 page was to be used for. I screamed at him as I described what he had just put me through, and I slammed the phone down in his ear. For the second time today, I had blown up at someone who cared about me. I felt sick.

Sandy and I met with our attorneys to discuss strategy. At one point during the meeting I totally lost it. The stress hit me like a brick wall, and I began sobbing. Stan, our attorney's assistant, and Sandy, did everything they could to comfort me. The fact that I broke down made our attorney very uncomfortable. I had been the strong one through all of this. I'm the one that chose to be vocal and to indict Brinkley by name in my earlier EEO filings. I'm the one that talked everyone else into filing complaints and taught them how to be tough. Now our attorney's "quarterback" was falling apart. I could feel him squirming in his skin. It made me feel weak and small. Our attorney left, and the rest of us continued the conversation. I kept thinking of how all of this was going to affect my kids and my parents. My parents were almost in their 80s and not in good health. This type of scandal, with me in the middle, could just kill them. I shared these concerns with Stan and Sandy.

Before I left our attorney's office, I called my husband and apologized. He apologized, too, and told me to hang in there and that he would be with me no matter what happened. When I told Stan about this, he reminded me of how lucky I was to have such a supportive husband. He was right.

On the way home, I began nodding off at the wheel. I was so tired. I pulled over at a mall off the I-10 freeway and dozed. I began to dream and suddenly I was at a black tie gala at what appeared to be the Shrine

Auditorium in L.A. I was standing in a large, beautiful foyer, and I saw the toddler outside at the entryway. He looked the same, came into the building and walked past me, smiling. I followed him to a staircase overlooking the large theater. There were hundreds of people there, all in formal attire. I noticed several famous people: Angie Dickinson, Gina Davis, Kevin Costner and Jay Leno, to name a few.

I looked down at the toddler and thought, as though he could read my mind, "Why have you brought me here? I don't want to be here. I want to go to the beautiful farm and see who that man is." He looked at me with his beautiful, entrancing eyes and nodded his head towards the edge of the stage. I began looking at the people there, and I noticed that one particular man stood out. His back was to me, but as I watched him, I knew it was the same young man that I had seen at the farm in my other dreams. He had on a black tuxedo and was holding something in his hand. I walked down the steps toward him trying to see his face. As I walked past the well-dressed people, an uncomfortable feeling swept over me. I felt like I didn't belong here, like I was caught eavesdropping on someone's conversation, like a fish out of water. I got as close as I could to the man before the toddler stopped me.

As I watched the young man from behind, I noticed that several people came up to him and shook his hand or gave him with that shallow Hollywood kiss common among rich socialites. He didn't seem particularly comfortable with this, but he was polite and dignified. He had brief conversations with people, and all the while appeared very stiff and uncomfortable in his tux. His hands mostly stayed folded in front of him squeezing a pack of cigarettes. His index finger twitched up and down. I could tell that he was here by necessity and was going to escape as soon as he had the chance. I heard his soft, deep voice with the accent. I wondered if his voice sounded like that because he smoked too much for too long. I tried to position myself to see his face, but I couldn't. Suddenly, he shifted his weight and turned his head slightly, allowing me to catch a glimpse of his left eye. The color of his eye took me by surprise. His eyes were the same deep, beautiful blue as the toddlers. I only noticed his eyes for a split second and wasn't able get a good look at his face, but again, I knew that he was a stranger to me, but a stranger to whom I felt some sort of connection. This connection was not in any way romantic, but somehow comforting and heart-warming.

I awoke from the dream, my mind racing with questions. Why was I at the Shrine Auditorium? I remembered that I had been at the Shrine Auditorium working the Bill and Hillary Clinton campaign as a cross-designated Secret Service Agent. A cross-designated Secret Service Agent is an agent from another Treasury agency (i.e. Customs, IRS, ATF) that had received Secret Service training and could be used to perform personal protection for the Secret Service. Every four years during the presidential campaign and for other manpower intensive events, these cross-designated agents are called upon to augment the Secret Service. I remembered seeing those same movie stars at this and other fund-raisers in Hollywood and Beverly Hills during the campaign. I remembered the highlight of that campaign was when my hero, Angie Dickinson, shook my hand and asked me how I liked being an agent. I shyly tipped my head down and said, "Fine, m'am." She looked me in the eye and said, "Myyyyyy, you're a pretty one; you're in the wrong line of work, sweetie." That was one of the most special moments in my life, one I'll never forget. When I was little, I use to pretend I was a police-woman like Angie Dickinson and here I was, shaking her hand and being complimented by her. She was gorgeous, and I only hope I look half that good when I'm her age.

My thoughts went back to my dream, and I wondered if my work with the Secret Service during the campaigns had some connection to all of this. I didn't remember anyone at any of the campaign sites looking like this man in my dreams. Why was this man there when he clearly didn't want to be? Maybe his profession required him to be there in the same way that mine did. Maybe he really wanted to be back at his beautiful farm with his cows, dogs and ducks just as much as I did. Why did the toddler take me there? Who was this guy? I tried and tried to recall his facial features, but all that stood out in my mind were his beautiful, blue eyes. Maybe he was the Angel of Death, and the toddler was my guardian angel. Maybe I was losing my mind.

Chapter Sixteen

The Other Side of the Lens

September 11, 1998, Ruben and I met at the shooting range. Going there actually helped me take my mind off things. I shot a 148 out of 150, my best ever. After the range, Ruben told me that he wanted me to come by his house so he could show me something. He asked Mike Conner, who was also at the range, to meet us there and whispered to me that he needed an unbiased witness. Mike was the pilot who turned my ex-boyfriend into IA for displaying my pictures. I thought of how ironic it was that here he was now, an unwitting witness to our lawsuits. Life is certainly full of strange, intertwined relationships between people.

We caravaned over to Ruben's house in Yucaipa. As we were turning down his street, Ruben pointed to the streetlights. I looked and could not believe what I was seeing. There were two cameras, not one, but two, on separate poles, covering both entrances to Ruben's house. Ruben, Mike and I got out and photographed the cameras. Mike was extremely surprised and commented, "Whoever put up these cameras should have notified you, Ruben, that they were watching a crook in your neighborhood." Ruben looked at me and smiled. Then he broke the news to Mike that the cameras were for him. I was sure that when I got home my streetlights would have cameras as well.

Ruben and I went back to the office and checked in. For the first time, it dawned on us that our phones were probably being monitored also, so we walked to a pay phone close by. I felt as though someone had broken into my home and stolen some important possession. In a way that was accurate. They were stealing my privacy and my life. Ruben and I called the Postal Inspector, Alexander Pierce, regarding the threatening letter and explained the things that had happened since. We were concerned that Pierce would think that we were just a couple of paranoid nuts. But he didn't. I think he really believed us. We called our attorney but were unable to reach him.

Our walk back to the office was full of tension and anguish. We agreed that our phones at home and at work were probably tapped. Ruben was laughing on the outside, but I could tell that this was all starting to get to him, too. Our armor was starting to show chinks, and I tried to control my fear.

I went home that night and looked for cameras around my house. As far as I could see, there were none there.

On the morning of September 14, I got a strange call from our "favorite" IA investigator, Terri Clay, who paged me to his cell phone. I didn't recognize the number and was very curious when I returned his call. When Mr. Clay answered the phone, I became very angry. Still, I noticed that his tone of voice was very different from the other times I had talked to him. He seemed almost meek and practically begged me to meet with him. In previous phone calls when he had asked me to meet with him, he had a seemingly arrogant and accusing tone of voice, quite a contrast to what I was hearing now.

I asked him, "What is this about, Terri?" He immediately stated, as if to put me to ease, "This isn't about you, I mean, you're not under investigation." I then responded, "I'm not meeting with you until I know what this is about. My attorney advised me not to go along with any more of your witch-hunts." "This is about something you may have heard someone say," he replied, "something someone may have told you." I thought, "Oh, now that really clears things up for me." Still, my curiosity got the better of me, so I asked him where he wanted to meet. He said that he would drive out to Riverside and meet me someplace close to my office. Now this was a change; I had always had to drive to Long Beach to the IA office for their inquisitions. They had never

Darlene and Ruben Sandoval at the firing range

Darlene qualifying with shotgun at firing range

offered to drive out here. This just heightened my curiosity. He pleaded with me not to tell any of my co-workers about this meeting. He assured me that he would explain why at our meeting.

I asked him, "What is this about, Terri?" He immediately stated, as if to put me to ease, "This isn't about you, I mean, you're not under investigation." I then responded, "I'm not meeting with you until I know what this is about. My attorney advised me not to go along with any more of your witch-hunts." "This is about something you may have heard someone say," he replied, "something someone may have told you." I thought, "Oh, now that really clears things up for me." Still, my curiosity got the better of me, so I asked him where he wanted to meet. He said that he would drive out to Riverside and meet me someplace close to my office. Now this was a change; I had always had to drive to Long Beach to the IA office for their inquisitions. They had never offered to drive out here. This just heightened my curiosity. He pleaded with me not to tell any of my co-workers about this meeting. He assured me that he would explain why at our meeting.

I agreed to meet with IA Clay for lunch on Wednesday, September 16. I didn't trust him, not knowing what the real purpose of this meeting was, so I told Ruben about the meeting. Ruben was going to sit in his car across the street, and I asked my longtime friend and hairdresser, Roberta Rossa, to be inside the restaurant to witness the meeting. Roberta was the only hairdresser I had ever been to who listened to how you wanted your hair and did it right. She was also one of the smartest gals I'd ever met. She would have made a great agent.

We met at a restaurant called Spoons next to our office. When I walked in, I saw Roberta near the bar area, and I saw Mr. Clay in the back towards the window. Roberta smiled at me as if to say, "Don't worry. I got you covered." I knew I could trust her. Even though she was not in law enforcement, I knew that instinctively she knew what to do. There are three types of professionals that seem to have a sixth sense: cops, shrinks and hairdressers.

As I sat down at the table, I noticed that Mr. Clay had selected a seat right next to the front window, a tactic commonly used by cops when someone outside is covering them. I was chuckling inside about the situation. Here we were, both with someone covering us, and both pretending to be meeting alone. What a joke. As I sat down I gave him a smirk and a headshake, as if to let him know how suspicious I was of his intentions. "OK, Clay," I said, "what's this all about?" He began by thanking me for coming alone because he didn't want any of my coworkers to know he was meeting with me. He then stated that he and his boss believed that their office, IA, was being used by someone in my office to harm me. I was thinking to myself, "No kidding, Sherlock. I'm dealing with a freaking rocket scientist!" He showed me a transcript that had been typed and mailed into their office anonymously. The transcript was constructed as though it were a tape-recorded conversation between someone at the air unit and me speaking about information on my ex-boyfriend. The transcript had the signature block of our Investigative Aid, Yolanda Rios. There was no signature, just her signature block. I knew that I had to conceal my anger just in case this was another of IA's stunts to get me to overreact and do something unprofessional.

I told Clay that this was bogus; this conversation never happened. Clay stated that their office was worried that someone had been illegally wire tapping my phone because of the way the transcript was written. I explained that I believed it was written by someone who knew that I had a court order and restraining orders allowing me to record conversations between my ex-boyfriend and me because of his previous threatening phone calls. This transcript was also written to make it appear as though I was illegally recording people not covered in my court order. It became immediately apparent to me that "Einstein" Clay hadn't figured this out yet, and only when I pointed out the obvious, did he get it. These are the type of agents that work in

IA. Serving a term in IA is the only way mediocre agents would ever get a promotion.

I expressed my feelings of utter frustration about this situation. I told him of my letter of disciplinary action and quoted the last paragraph of this letter: "If circumstances change, this letter may be removed from your personnel file by local management." He rolled his eyes and shook his head in disbelief at someone being stupid enough to put this type of language in a letter like this. "For what ever reason, someone is trying to …" "Mess with me," I finished. He nodded his head yes. I stared into his eyes to see if he would break eye contact with me and turn his head (body language is a clue to someone's insincerity). He kept steady eye contact as I tried to read him, and he seemed surprisingly sincere.

I then made a suggestion to him: he shouldn't be meeting with me alone anymore. If he was in fact uninvolved in all this and was just caught in the middle as he had indicated, he should ask to be removed from investigating me anymore. I suggested that the next time he is asked to investigate Ruben, Sandy or myself, all of whom have lawsuits pending, to just try to get out of it and see what happens. He gave me a funny look, as if to say, "I don't get it." I told him to think about it.

As we were walking out, two people I knew were sitting in the bar area. They smiled and waved at me. They were the folks who owned the 76 Station where I always took my G-Ride for an oil and lube change. I waved back and noticed that Mr. Clay was giving me a funny look. He assumed that I had asked these people to cover this meeting and that I wanted him to know that they were there, that I had witnesses. I began to chuckle. I thought it ironic that he was drawing the correct conclusion about the wrong people! If he only knew that it was Roberta and not they!

On September 16, 1998, all SAIC, RAIC and Supervisor personnel from the SAIC/LA and the SAIC/San Diego were required to attend a management conference held in the Palm Springs area. The conference centered around a class entitled "Dealing with Problem Employees." A private attorney and former employee of the U.S. Customs Office of Regional Council taught this class. My good friend Ricardo Sandoval attended.

When he got back from the conference, Ricardo briefed Sandy and me over the phone. He told us that Evantie had cut him down in front of everybody, and they had exchanged verbal digs. I could tell Ricardo really hated Evantie. I explained to him that Evantie was doing management's dirty work for them. Evantie was one of Brinkley's stooges and was trying to give everyone the perception that the RAIC/Riverside and Ricardo's office, RAIC/Calexico, weren't getting along because of how Ricardo was handling things. Evantie was purposely undermining the relationship between the two offices in an effort to make Ricardo look bad. Ricardo and Sandy agreed that I was probably right in my assessment.

I thought about just how amazing it was that a handful of people, or even one person, could falsely alter the perceptions of others when they wanted to undermine someone. I had heard so many stupid rumors about Ricardo Sandoval and how he only got his promotion because he filed a lawsuit and that he was really incompetent. This was ludicrous but very familiar to me. I remembered hearing so much negative gossip about Hillary Clinton when Bill was first running for office. I had heard from dozens of men about how she was a real "ball buster," and that they had heard from "them" that she was a bitch to Secret Service Agents and a real political climber. Of course these rumors always came from the "them" zone; you know those mystical people who disperse information that conveniently fits the agenda of the person spreading the gossip. I was a "die-hard" Republican (Ronald Reagan was my hero), and there was a part of me that very stupidly believed all the gossip because it comfortably aligned with my political beliefs.

Then I was fortunate to be assigned to protect Hillary Clinton as an adjunct Treasury agent or OTA (Other Treasury Agents) during Bill's first and second campaign. I was amazed. After every negative thing that

I had heard about Hillary, what I saw with my own two eyes surprised me. I wasn't assigned directly to her jump team, but I did have the opportunity to observe her numerous times in and out of the public eye. She was nothing like what all of these men, and the obvious male chauvinists in the "they" zone, had described. She was a very professional, demure and soft-spoken woman. She was always warm and friendly toward the Treasury agents, and not once did I see her acting in any way like the ball-busting bitch "they" had portrayed her to be. She spent a lot of time working very hard on health care issues with her staff and seemed very sincere about her work. My dad always taught me that right, wrong, or indifferent people will judge you by the company you keep. Well, I had the opportunity to communicate frequently with members of Hillary's staff who were mostly female. They, too, were very nice, warm, professional ladies, who never came off as overbearing.

From what I saw, Hillary kept good company, and I was surprisingly impressed. I learned something very important from this and from Ricardo's situation: the "theys" of the world use gossip to undermine people they are afraid of. It is a subversive, cowardly tool to enhance the perpetrator's agenda. It is a tactic I would be on guard against after that.

My attention then turned back to our three-way conversation, and Sandy, Ricardo and I shared feelings of how the stress of the retaliation we had all received was affecting our lives, at home and at work. Ricardo confided in us that he went to the gym almost every night in the same way that I did to relieve stress. We shared with each other how this was impacting our marriages and causing stress on our families. The conversation strayed to the dangers of the job and how all of this was in many ways more stressful than the times that we had almost been blown up. I thought about my strange dreams, and I asked him if he believed in guardian angels. I was surprised by the following story that Ricardo shared with us.

Darlene with President Ronald Reagan

Ricardo was working a dope deal deep undercover, south of the border in Tijuana (TJ). The deal went south (cop slang for a deal going bad), and the crooks thought Ricardo was trying to rip them off. They kidnapped him, but somehow, he convinced them that he was about to get a large sum of money. They only had to take him into TJ, and his girlfriend would get the money. This was all a lie, and Ricardo was just trying to stall for time any way he could to stay alive until the surveillance team found him. Ricardo was wired up during the whole thing. The crooks took him into TJ, parked the car in a shopping mall parking lot, and told Ricardo to stay in the car. The crooks exited the car leaving Ricardo alone. All of a sudden, a strange Latino male, not one of the crooks that Ricardo had been dealing with, got into the car and sat next to him. The guy said, "Hey, buddy, just calm down. You're going to make it through this, but you got to calm down and clear your head." Ricardo said that they conversed for several minutes and then the guy got out just as federal agents were surrounding the car, the crooks and Ricardo. The guy had just disappeared, and no one else had seen him. Ricardo didn't know how on earth the guy could have gotten past all of the federal agents with their guns drawn. Sandy asked Ricardo if he had ever listened to the tape of it. Ricardo answered, "You know, that's the strangest thing. I did, and all you can hear in the conversation is my voice."

I was taken aback by his story. Ricardo is a very sincere man and was not one to make this kind of thing up or imagine it. I wanted so badly to share my recurring dream with he and Sandy, but I lacked the confidence. I was afraid that they would think I was nuts, but Ricardo's story did make me much more comfortable with my dreams. Maybe these dreams did mean something and the toddler and the man were somehow trying to help me.

On September 23, 1998, I got a call from Tom Best who was at his UP office. He had profiled five or six tanker cars and was setting them up to be weighed. I briefed our new Group Supervisor, O'Shea, and he seemed somewhat enthusiastic. Evantie tried to pull me off the project again, but no one else in the office had the expertise or the desire to deal with this. So, I was back on for now, but it was made very clear that it was only temporary. Evantie clearly hated the fact that he had no choice but to put me back in the rail yards. Best, Ervin Rios and I began running all the leads and pulling all the entry information on the cars. As I started down this long tanker car road again, part of me wanted to put in for sick leave and pawn this mess off on someone else. I wanted to stick it to Evantie the way he had stuck it to me and leave him with no one qualified to control this railcar fiasco. I knew it wouldn't matter how well I did, how much dope I seized, or how many people I put in jail, I would not get any credit for a job well done. And even worse, others less qualified than I would be promoted over me. This was the first time I recall feeling this way about my work. I felt so burnt, but I did my job anyway.

September 25, 1998, the SAIC/LA had their annual awards ceremony and picnic at a park in Long Beach. Ruben and I went together and had agreed to meet Sandy, Paige Yates (our mole under Brinkley's nose at the SAIC office) and the rest of the "trouble-makers" there. We thought it might be fun for Brinkley to see us all together eating his free food. Just before we left the office for this gala event, I got a call from Chief Inspector Jeremy O'Leary. O'Leary was working on the rail project with me. He and I teamed up because of all of the trouble I was having tracking railroad cars and their cargo in my two cases, Operation Black Widow and Operation Tanker Car. O'Leary called with some terrific ideas on how to get funding for the current suspect tanker cars I was going to have to open on Monday. It cost a lot of money to have a contract company examine these tanker cars. This was the end of the fiscal year for government funding, and the RAIC/Riverside was out of money. I liked O'Leary's ideas but had no authority to do anything about them. So I asked O'Leary to talk to my RAIC, Evantie, about extending my stay on the rail project, and he agreed.

As Brinkley was talking to Evantie, Ruben and I left for the picnic. We only stayed for about an hour, ate and left. We didn't stay for the awards ceremony, and I'm glad we didn't. Once again, everyone else in my office was recognized for his or her work for the year, and I received nothing. I don't know why I was surprised. By this time, I should have expected it. I guess I thought that the tanker car case, as the biggest seizure in our office, was so significant–significant enough for the Acting Commissioner of Customs to call me and thank me for all of my work, significant enough that Janet Reno was closely watching the case – that even Brinkley wouldn't be dumb enough to overlook it, but he did. Even people in my office who hadn't done anything for years were recognized for something. But here I had the second most significant case of the year for the entire agency, and I didn't even get honorable mention. My case was only second to Operation Casablanca, an international, undercover, money laundering operation that was, coincidentally, targeting the same organization I was targeting in my tanker car case.

Brinkley's stunt had the desired effect; I was crushed. The good news was that he'd never know he had hurt me so. I had several agents—Bob Mattivi, Ruben Sandoval and Sandy Nunn—tell me that this was, again, a real slap in the face. Everyone knew the significance of the tanker car case and knew that it was a real farce that I received no recognition for it. I came home, cried, called Sam at our attorney's office and relayed the story to him. He tried to console me in the same way that everyone else did: "Don't worry, this will only help your lawsuit." For some reason this didn't make me feel any better, but I did learn something from this. I now knew just how far my RAIC, Lawrence Evantie, and SAIC, Drake Brinkley, would go on this playing field. It was clear that Evantie was actively carrying out Brinkley's plans for us because it was Evantie's responsibility to put me in for an award, and he didn't.

Here I was dealing with five more tanker cars, supposedly loaded with dope, and Evantie was using my talents, and all the while, stabbing me in the back. If that wasn't enough, I received a call from Ervin Rios.

Ervin told me that after Chief O'Leary had his conversation with Evantie earlier that day, O'Leary called Ervin to relay the gist of the conversation. Evidently, while O'Leary was attempting to offer help on these tanker cars to Evantie, Evantie was very negative and made it clear that he didn't want Inspection and Control involved. He also told O'Leary that they were considering taking me off of this case and didn't want me involved in the Operation Lite Rail project. O'Leary tried to reason with Evantie and attempted to explain to him how necessary it was that I be involved in this project, but this, of course, was to no avail. When O'Leary point blank asked Evantie why I wasn't going to be allowed to participate in Operation Lite Rail and why I was being taken off of the case, Evantie answered, "It's just politics."

How ludicrous! I was taught in the military that the mission comes first, then your men, and your needs come last. In Customs, managers raise a moistened finger in the air to see which way the political wind is blowing before they make a decision. The Customs management philosophy is to decide first what political best interest is served and then how their personal best interest can be served by using the political best interest as their vehicle. Then they consider how the mission might be accomplished without damaging their political best interests. And the troops ... well, the troops are simply cannon fodder to serve the interest of corrupt managers and their politics.

Chapter Seventeen

Depositions

October 2, 1998, the U.S. Attorneys office in Ruben Sandoval's case deposed me. The U.S. Attorney's office represents U.S. Customs in civil lawsuits. The AUSA on this case was one who had worked in the criminal division. I was grilled under oath for over eight hours. When it was all over, I had a sense of relief. I felt good that all of their scare tactics had failed, and I had done my duty by telling the truth about what happened to Ruben, Sandy and I. I felt professional again. I felt a sense of cleansing by standing up to adversity with dignity and honor. I told the truth no matter what the consequences might be.

On October 7, 1998, our attorneys in Ruben's federal case deposed SAIC Brinkley. Brinkley lied and denied that he made any statements about dealing with any complaints generated from the RAIC/Riverside during the November 1996 promotion party. Additionally, Brinkley stated that he had nothing to do with the assignment of vehicles to agents.

The same day, SSA Peter Blake was also deposed on the same case. In this deposition Blake confirmed that he had attended this promotion party and that Brinkley did in fact make comments about dealing with complainants at the RAIC/Riverside. When asked whether he and Edwin Easel had taken heroin home overnight, Blake lied under oath and denied this accusation.

Two days later Ruben and I were loaned out to RAIC/Orange County (RAIC/OC) for a series of search warrants. We arrived at RAIC/OC that morning for the briefing and found that Peter Blake was the case agent delivering the briefing. When we walked into the room there were already about 30 agents and TFO's present. Ruben grabbed a donut and some coffee, and we sat down. Blake looked up and saw Ruben and I glaring at him. In fact, if looks could kill, he'd be dead. I thought to myself, "What a lying weasel." Blake quickly broke eye contact, and his face turned red with embarrassment. I said under my breath, "coward." Ruben kicked my in the shins under the table and said, "Shh, hothead."

On our way home from executing the warrants, we hit typical southern California rush-hour traffic, giving Ruben and I a chance to brainstorm. We were irate that Blake had committed perjury and would probably get away with it. I asked Ruben if he was still the alternate evidence custodian, and he said he was. I asked him if he could get into the evidence locker that night and look at the logs. He stated that he really wasn't supposed to be in there without the authority of the primary evidence custodian, David Gray. I asked him if he had ever looked at the logs to see if they failed to cover their tracks on the heroin incident. Ruben said, "No, but nobody's that dumb, Dar. You know they covered themselves in the logs." "Don't underestimate how incredibly dumb these people really are," I said. After some convincing, Ruben and I proceeded to the RAIC/Riverside and entered the evidence room. Much to Ruben's surprise, the log clearly showed that the heroin had not gone back to the evidence room until the evening of the next day. As Ruben and I high-fived each other I said, "I told you so!"

We photocopied the evidence log. While Ruben was busy copying, I pulled SA Janet Somers' case file on this heroin case and found her 9-B's (case chronology form) showing that she had briefed Winkowsky on the heroin incident and shared her concerns about her criminal case. I photocopied these, too. We picked up the phone and contacted the on-call IA duty agent and reported it. Ruben faxed the logs to him, and we could both smell justice in the air, and I could see joy on Ruben's face. I slept well that night.

On October 13, 1998, our attorneys in Ruben's federal lawsuit deposed SSA Jerry Johnston. During the deposition Jerry was asked the following question: "Did Supervisor Ivan Winkowsky have a problem with women in law enforcement?" Before he could answer this question, the AUSA representing Customs, Tim Deer, stopped the deposition and asked Jerry to step outside. Jerry and Deer stepped into the hall where Deer directed Jerry not to answer the question. Jerry was a prior military officer, a fellow Kentuckian and a very honorable agent. He looked at Deer in disbelief and went back into the deposition. Our attorney asked Jerry the question again, and Jerry, in a very clear and determined tone of voice, told the truth: Winkowsky did have a problem with women.

On October 13, 1998, AUSA Deer issued a letter, essentially a gag order, to U.S. Customs. It was directed to all U.S. Customs employees specifically regarding SA Sandoval's civil litigation against Customs. The memo was sent by fax and Federal Express, addressed to SAIC Drake Brinkley. The memo directed Customs management to "Please advise your employees accordingly." My mole at the SAIC office, Paige Yates, who was right under Brinkley's nose, got me a copy of the document. There's a term for Mr. Deer's behavior: witness tampering.

The next day, Jerry Johnston told me about his deposition and what had happened. I could tell it was important to him that I knew that he has done the right thing and had told the truth. I gave him a hug and said, "Was there ever any doubt? Well done, my Kentucky Pizanno." Jerry and I had very similar, almost parallel, lives. We were both military officers, we were both from Kentucky, and somehow, we ended up in the same office together. Jerry's integrity was firmly intact, and I knew that he would say the right thing under pressure. I was proud of him.

On October 14, 1998, ASAIC Donald Chin, under oath during deposition, confirmed suspicions that pre-selection, a practice against OPM regulations, was definitely involved in the selection process of late 1996 when Ruben and I were passed over. On most everything else, Chin played dumb. Chin worked directly under Brinkley, and to no one's surprise, he retired shortly after this deposition.

On November 10, 1998, Ruben Sandoval sent a letter to the Customs Commissioner, Raymond Kelly, regarding the lack of investigation by IA into the mishandling of evidence (heroin) and subsequent cover up. We were sure that Kelly would either ignore it completely or simply sick his IA dogs on us again. Either way, we wanted to ensure that we documented that he had, in fact, been informed and couldn't play ignorant down the road.

On December 9, 1998, the Director of the Office of Internal Affairs, Harrison Wells, notified SA Sandoval that his office would not be investigating this matter. His letter stated that IA cannot investigate itself and that the investigation would be referred to the U.S. Treasury Department, Office of the Inspector General (commonly referred to by most agents as the blackhole – everything gets buried and nothing gets done). Harrison Wells was himself currently being investigated by a grand jury on corruption charges brought against him related to the whistleblowing of RAIC/Calexico, Ricardo Sandoval. Drake Brinkley had placed Wells in the position of Director of IA when Brinkley was the Director of the Customs Office of Investigations (the Special Agents). I guess it takes a crook to promote a crook.

Chapter Eighteen

Wake Up and Smell the Corruption

On January 17, 1999, I got a call from Tom Best at UP Railroad. He told me that he had five more tanker cars sitting in his yard, manifested and empty, and all of them were five to nine tons over weight. I told him that I had been taken off of the rail project. "Well, who the hell am I supposed to call?" he exclaimed. Nobody else over there knows this stuff, and I don't want to talk to anyone else." I replied, "All right Tom, what are the numbers?" He gave me the car numbers, and I pulled the entries from the Customs Computers. Just as I feared, the Customs general hold that I had previously placed in the system had already been released. Once again, if it hadn't been for the alertness of Tom Best, the cars would not have been brought back to the Colton rail yard.

Bob Mattivi was the Acting Group Supervisor at the time. Bob was a super agent. He had made some of the most famous cases in Customs and had been my mentor when I first came on the job. I trusted Bob and decided to show him what we had found on the tanker cars. I called Best back and asked him to bring the routes of the cars (printouts from the UP computer system displaying the routes of railcars after they entered the U.S.). When Best arrived, we looked at the routes of the cars. It looked very suspicious. They were manifested as empty. Railroads invoice their customers by weight and distance, making it more cost effective for the customer to route their cars in the most direct manner possible. These cars had been imported from Baja, Mexico, routed through Texas and Arizona, and then sent to Colton, California. This made no sense and would not be cost effective for the shipper or customer. The manifest also had stamped on it, "NO WEIGHT PER WEIGH AGREEMENT." Shippers will often have a standing account set up with the major railroads and are invoiced to their credit line. The accounts can be set up to prepay the routes at the max cost, assuming the weight will be at the maximum. This saves the shipper the expense of having to pay the route (distance) cost of having the cars sent to a weight location to be weighed. When this occurs, the manifest will be stamped "NO WEIGHT PER WEIGH AGREE-MENT." This method is not, however, normally done for empty cars. Why would you prepay for a full car when the car is empty? And it is never done on pressurized tanker cars. Tanker cars, due to my rail project and Customs holds, have to be shipped to a weigh station anyway, and the shipper eats the cost of the extra distance as the price of doing business, compliments of the U.S. Customs Service.

The way these cars were routed and manifested made no sense. Best and I briefed Mattivi. Mattivi seemed pleased and said, "Well, Dar, it looks like you guys may have gotten yourself another big load. Let me go brief Evantie and …" I interrupted Mattivi and said, "Woah, Bob, before you go up there, there's something you should know. I don't want you to get blindsided with anything. Bob, Evantie pulled me off the rail project and told me to stay away from there. If you go in there with this, Evantie's going to throw a fit." Bob looked at me like I was crazy and said, "Oh come on, Darlene, no he won't. You're just being sensitive because of all the crap that you and Ruben are going through. Besides, who else am I going to send? Everyone else is in training, and you're the only one who knows this stuff." He smiled at me with his sweet, wise smile, as if to say, "Just trust your old mentor," and he took the documentation to Evantie's office.

After a few seconds, Best and I heard Evantie yelling at Bob. Several minutes later, Mattivi returned to the back of the office where we were waiting for him. He tossed the documents down on the table in front of us in disgust. He sat down, looked at Best with a look of total bewilderment. "I don't know what to say. I don't know what to tell you guys. He wouldn't even entertain the idea of having them pressure tested at no cost to the government. This is ridiculous!"

I had been sitting there leaning back with my feet propped up on the table drinking a bottle of water. I brought my feet to the floor, tossed my water-bottle in the trash in disgust and asked, "Now do you believe me, Bob?" Mattivi answered, "I don't know what to believe, and I'm embarrassed to say this, but Darlene, stay away from this." I could tell by the look of anguish on his face that Bob was concerned for me, disturbed by Evantie's reaction and totally stumped as to what to do. This was the first time I had seen Mattivi at a loss for a quick-witted answer. Mattivi was a sharp, confident, seasoned veteran who was never at a loss for what to do. His reaction scared me. I got up and walked Best to his car. "What's going on here Darlene?" he asked. "Is someone corrupt here or what?" I shook my head in embarrassment and disgust, looked down at the ground, and said, "Best, you know it ain't me." "No, I know it isn't you, Dar. You're the only one that I've been able to deal with over here, but something about this just doesn't look right Darlene, and you know it." I looked up at him and said, "Best, I don't know what to do." He just shook my hand and ended the conversation by saying, "Hey, we'll have to get together and talk about this later." Five days later, the tanker cars were released without so much as even a pressure test being done which would have been no cost to the government. Five suspect pressurized tanker cars five to nine tons over weight, manifested as empty, were released against policy and reached their destinations, a rail spur somewhere in downtown L.A. With all of the red flags we had, those cars should have never been released without at least being pressure tested.

I met Ruben and Renado the day the cars were released and told them what had happened. Renado couldn't believe it. "Darlene, this thing is getting dangerous. I'm telling you, I've said it once and I'll say it again, this stuff has nothing to do with the EEO crap you guys are dealing with. I think you've wandered into some serious corruption in your agency, and that Brinkley guy is in it up to his nose. Or maybe it's some type of CIA undercover crap or something." Renado began looking around in an animated, paranoid fashion as if he were looking for somebody about to get him and said jokingly, "Geez! I'm gonna get the hell away from you guys, the red dot could appear on your forehead any minute." We all laughed, and I said, "Yeah, there you go again, that 'you guys' line. Renado, face it, you're in this, dude." Renado responded, "Oh, no I'm not." He pulled out his badge and pointed at it and said, "You see this here, it says San Bernardino Police Department, not Department of Treasury." Then I pulled out my badge, pointed at it and said, "Oh, you mean U.S. Corruptions." We all burst out laughing, but when the laughter stopped, I could see the concern on their faces.

I knew Renado was just kidding us. I knew he would never let us down. The man knew what the word loyalty meant. I thought of how Renado reminded me so much of one of my NCOIC's (Non-Commissioned Officer In Charge) in the military. His name was William Watson, but we called him Little Willie for short. Little Willie was six feet, three inches tall, and was about 300 pounds of pure muscle (similar to Renado's build, but taller). I remembered one time when I was a young lieutenant and the duty officer, I got a call in the middle of the night from one of my MP's (Military Police). In a very panicked voice over the radio I heard, "Hey, L.T. (short for lieutenant), you'd better get out here. We got a wild man. I need help." I jumped into the car with Willie and we sped out to the west gate of the post in the middle of nowhere.

When we arrived, there were two marked units and four of my MP's were surrounding the crazy man. We got out of the unit, and one of the MP's ran over to us. "What's going on?" I asked. "What's this guy's problem?" The MP was out of breath and his wire-rimmed glasses had been smashed on his face. He caught his breath and said, "I'm not sure L.T., but I think he's got rabies." "Rabies!" I exclaimed. We had been having a rabies epidemic on the post that summer. There had been several rabid skunks, squirrels and even domestic cats killed by animal control. They had been giving out warnings for the past several weeks describing the signs of rabies and suggesting having pets inoculated. I looked at the guy and sure enough, he was foaming at the mouth, swatting at everyone and growling like a madman. The MP showed me that he had already broken through two sets of handcuffs and put bite marks in MP Cochran's jump boots. I realized that if this guy bit, scratched or slobbered on us we would have to get those god-forsaken rabies shots, and even those weren't 100% effective. Willie looked at me and said, "L.T., we can't risk the lives of our men. We're gonna have to shoot this guy. Ma'am, rabies is potentially fatal, and this is a life threatening situation that calls for deadly force." When he said this, my face dropped. I was only a whopping 23 years old. I knew when I entered law enforcement that someday I might be faced with having to kill someone, but this was not how I pictured it.

Willie saw the terrified look on my face and laughed. He walked to the rear of his car and said, "Don't worry, L.T., I got you covered." He pulled a tire iron out of his trunk and walked over to me and the other MP. "I need you two to distract him from the front," he instructed, "so I can get a whack at him from the back." The MP and I pulled our nightsticks and began distracting him as Willie had suggested. We would poke at him with the sticks from a safe distance only to have him lunge at us. Willie was working his way around him when the madman lunged at me. I fell backwards over a rock and the man ran at me. I could see his evil, crazed eyes as he was ready to pounce on me. It was one of the most horrible things I have ever seen. Just as the lunatic was on top of me, Willie whacked his scull with the tire iron. He dropped down almost on top of me, slobber dripping from his mouth onto my uniform. I jumped up in terror and ran to my vehicle, grabbed a piece of cloth lying on the seat and desperately tried to wipe the slobber off. The next day we found out that the madman did not have rabies but had been on PCP. When I heard this, my heart dropped. I thought,

Darlene conducting training as Captain in the U.S. Army M.P. Corps

Darlene teaching water survival training in the Army

"Oh my gosh! I almost ordered this man shot, and he didn't have rabies." I will always remember Willie's quick thinking and be grateful for him saving my ass. I had the same kind of warm loyalty towards Renado. He had saved Ruben's and my skin more times than I can count.

On February 8, 1999, I was out on surveillance when I got a 911 page from Ruben. I knew if Ruben used 911, it was serious. I called him on the cell phone, and he told me that he was called into Lewis' office where he was informed that the next morning he had to drive to San Diego to be interviewed by Internal Affairs. Ruben tried to make his voice sound confident, but I could sense the fear and anger. He asked me if I could meet him and Renado for lunch, and I did.

We met at a little hole-in-the-wall Mexican place that Renado and Ruben liked. It was a real low-key place, and we were not likely to bump into IA. Renado greeted me with his usual bear hug, but Ruben looked depressed and worried. When I shook his hand he squeezed my hand hard and stared deep into my eyes as though he wanted me to know he was covering up his pain with a tough exterior. I shook my head, and said, "F–ing fools!" Ruben said, "Renado, can you believe that she kisses our friend Ben with that mouth," to which I replied, "I only get like this around you guys. You're a bad influence." We all laughed.

Renado just kept shaking his head as we updated him on the latest. He kept saying, "Darlene, this is about the tanker car case, I'm telling you! You were never supposed to find that dope. You messed up somebody's action. They wouldn't go to these extremes to come after you guys over an EEO complaint. I'm telling you. You know it, and I know it! This is some serious stuff here, and even your prosecutor Yvette is worried. I'm telling you, you guys are in danger, you guys are in danger!" "Wait a minute," I replied. "What do you mean 'you guys?' I seem to recall that you were out there with me, every step of the way, amigo, crawling all over those cars. You mean *we* are in danger." Renado responded, "I don't think so little missy, there ain't no IA investigations or surveillance on me, not yet anyways." Renado's laughter faded, and I could see the fear on his face as he continued, "I'm telling you, what you guys put together with Rios paints a very scary picture. This isn't just about your EEO fight. You stumbled right into a huge mess. You picked up a rock that you weren't supposed to see under." As I thought about what Renado said, my stomach started burning. I wasn't sure if it was from the fear of what I had gotten us into, or the incredibly bad food Ruben kept making me eat at this place. That night I swam a mile in 57 minutes and ran three miles before going home to my kids. I just could not take this anger home with me; my family deserved better than this.

That night when I got home, my husband Ben remarked, "You were at the gym for a long time. What happened at work today?" I told him what happened and what Renado thought about the situation. I saw fear on my husband's face. He said in a low, serious voice, "I want you, Sandy and Ruben to quit digging into this tanker car stuff." Ben's fear turned quickly to anger when I didn't respond. He grabbed my shoulders, looked me dead in the eye and said, "What are you, crazy? You're going to get us all killed! I saw on the news what they did to those people in Matamoras, (referring to the 1999 slaying of the 21 men, women, and children murdered in Matamoras, Mexico by suspected members of the Arellano-Felix Drug Cartel) and that's the same organization you're going after!" I broke away from him. "What the hell do you expect me to do? This is my job!" Ben responded, "That part isn't! Not that in-house corruption stuff you all are going after. Look, just do your criminal case, and leave the rest of this crap alone, please, Darlene, please. Our kids need their mom, and Ruben's kids need him." At dinner, Ben looked at all of the kids and then looked at me and said, "This is what's important, sweety, this."

On February 9, 1999, Ruben made his journey to San Diego. I tried to go with him, but he wouldn't let me. This was his attempt at showing some kind of control over the situation. When I went into the office I passed by that little snake, Edwin Easel. He had an arrogant smirk on his face as if to say, "Ha, ha, Ruben's getting his now, isn't he? And you're next." As he walked past me with his smirk I said, "Well, girly boy, did your kids pick out your wardrobe today? That's some gay shirt you got on there." This was my weak attempt at wiping the sneer off his little face without hitting him upside the head with my tennis racket (kept in office for play at lunch). Easel replied with, "Ha, ha, ha, how mature of you, Darlene." "Weasel, why don't you run into Evantie's office and suck up to him. Maybe he'll spoon-feed you another case." Yolanda, our office Investigative Aid, saved me by interrupting and saying, "Hey, both of you, pipe down right now or I'll kick both of your asses." I knew not to tangle with Yolanda. Yolanda was a New York Puerto Rican that really could make good on her threat. She was my friend, an incredibly sharp lady who had her integrity in the right place. She knew what had been going on, and she resented it. She, too, had demonstrated a spine, and when it came time for her to be interviewed by the EEO and IA investigators, she came forward and told the truth at great risk. I was grateful for her courage, and I was grateful to her for the save between Easel the Weasel and me.

I went into the kitchen and got a Mountain Dew. I hadn't slept the night before. I was worried and still fuming about what was going to happen to Ruben. I can always count on Mountain Dew to keep me on the go. I passed Yolanda in the hall and she pulled me back into the kitchen and asked, "A Mountain Dew this early in the morning and taking on Easel the Weasel? What's going on, Darlene?" I told her briefly about my situation, and she was visibly concerned. She put her arm around me and said, "Listen, girlfriend, you've got to not react to this stuff. This little episode in the hall here is just what they want. They know you have a temper, and they are using Ruben and Sandy to get to you. They ain't got nothing on you they can come after you with, so they are pushing your buttons. Just chill lady, just chill." I gave Yolanda a big hug, thanked her for the good advice and headed back to my office. As I drank my Dew, it was like I had taken a shot of whiskey, and I could feel it burn all the way down my throat. I wanted to vomit.

I made a weak attempt at completing some reports, but I kept making mistakes. I was tired from lack of sleep, worried and anxious because I hadn't heard from Ruben, and sick to my stomach from the stress and the Dew. I completed some packing in the office as we were moving our office from the northeastern part of the City of Riverside to Downtown Riverside, close to the courthouse. We had been loading a moving van all day long and carrying things over to the new office. Most of us were sad to leave the old office. We had a lot of good times there and a lot of great memories. At lunchtime, we all had a little celebration to say good-bye to the old office. There were a couple of bottles of wine involved and a lot of good food. I, of course, had my husband, "Chef Ben," prepare something fabulous.

As the afternoon grew, I took special note that one of our more decadent and loose agents, Sherry King, was getting plastered alongside of David Gray. Sherry was the kind of female agent who does more damage to the reputation of women in the work place than most male chauvinists. Sherry had an affair with one of our former RAIC's, the boss of our field office, Jim Wilson, and everyone knew about it. They weren't exactly what you would call discrete. We all knew Jim Wilson's wife and liked her very much. Wilson's actions had caused a morale problem in the office and lessened his own credibility. Sherry displayed her disgusting behavior on a silver platter, available for use as ammunition by male chauvinists in their broad brushing of all women in the work place.

I noticed that Sherry was not only plastered, but that Gray had loaded her and her glass of wine in his G-ride and transported her to the new office. She was so plastered that everyone noticed, and I'm confident that Evantie knew, too. I was also sure that no manager would say anything or report the two of them for their behavior, especially Gray. I found this appalling. Gray was instrumental in going after Ruben for the incident about having his children in the G-ride, yet here Gray was transporting a drunken female agent, and her alcohol, in his G-ride. What a hypocrite!

As I sat there observing this fiasco and wondering how to handle it, the phone rang. It was Sandy asking if I had heard anything. I told her I hadn't. She sensed I was really worried and stated, "This is just such crap. The bright side of this is that these stupid jerks are just proving our point and making us one hell of a lawsuit. Don't worry, Darlene, Ruben's smart; he'll keep his cool, and he will be all right. I'm sure that he'll call us when they're done with him." Sandy's a great gal. She always tried to make me feel better when I needed it most. I told her of what I had just observed between Gray and Sherry King. She told me that I should definitely report it to IA to see if they would lift a finger to go after one of their fellow goons. I knew she was right.

I told her she better cool it or she would be giving them phony ammunition to come after her. I also told her about what Ben had said about our extracurricular internal corruption investigation and about how I'd lost it with Easel the Weasel in the hall. When I got off of the phone with Sandy, I felt bad about causing her more concern, she's got her share of troubles and doesn't need me to be chastising her. Here she called to be supportive, and all I did was run her down. I felt like such a moron.

At 1500hrs, I gave up on my quest for report writing, I was just making a mess of things. I went to the gym and swam. About halfway through my swim, I had to get out of the pool, go to the bathroom and throw up all the Dew I drank. I finished my mile but lost track of my time. When I went to my locker to change, I found a message from Ruben on my pager. I called him up and he asked me to meet him and Renado at the usual hole-in-the-wall.

When I got there, the guys were already at our table. My hair was still wet from swimming and showering, and they made jokes about it as if to mask their worry about what was happening. Renado asked me how my training for the Police Olympics was going. Ruben interrupted, "Are you kidding me? That's all she does now. I can't get any work out of her anymore. All she does is run and swim!" They both laughed, and I said, "Yea, yea, yea, yuck it up, you turkeys."

"OK, enough fun at my expense. Spill it, Ruben. What happened?" I asked. He explained, "It's that F-ing Weasel Easel!" As Ruben said that, I kicked him in the chins under the table. Ruben grabbed his leg and yelled, "Ow! What was that for?" "You kiss your wife and kids with that mouth!" I said. Renado laughed. Ruben said, "As I was saying, before I was rudely interrupted, Weasel ratted me out about something that happened six or seven years ago. I had my kids in my G-ride because I had to drop them off at the sitters. We got a call on a load, and I didn't have a car to take them as mine was in the shop, and I didn't have time to take them, drop them off, and then come back and get my G-ride anyway. I picked Weasel up first, so, of course, he saw this." Renado said, "That's it? Unbelievable!" I reminded them of how if Easel was just coming forward with this information now, then he, too, should be in trouble for failure to report Ruben in a timely fashion.

I then told them about what had just happened with Gray transporting a very drunk King and her alcohol in Gray's G-ride. I told them I was going to report it and demand that Gray come under the same fire as Ruben. Ruben looked at me out of the corner of his eye with a smirk on his face, and said "Yeah, right." Renado joined in, "Yeah, they're not going to go after their boy, oh no, nuh uh." I responded with, "Yeah, but IA's unwillingness to go after Weasel for not reporting the Ruben/G-ride incident in a timely manner and Gray for the Sherry King drunk episode, demonstrates that IA is engaging in selective enforcement of Customs policies. They are proving us right—that IA is the Goon Squad for Customs' corrupt management."

Ruben put up a good front as he continued telling us of his grilling by IA. He told the story almost as though he was reading it from a report, detached and unemotional, but I could see the stress on his face. I knew what this would do to him financially if they gave him the maximum punishment of 45 days off with no pay. Ruben had been through a divorce and had had to fight for custody of his kids several times over the past couple of years. With his new wife and baby, and now this, I knew it would just about break him financially. As I sat there listening to him, I withheld my concern. I wanted to cry, but instead, I made stupid jokes and funny insults. Inside, I just felt ill.

That night I told Ben what was going on. He just could not believe what was happening to us. He saw how worried I was and attempted to put me at ease by taking me to the movies to get my mind off of things. After the movies we had a good talk. Ben said, "I can see the stress getting to you, Darlene. It's affecting us, it's affecting our sex life, and it's wearing you down. I'm not blaming you, and I think that you are doing the best you can. If it weren't for your workout sessions, I'm sure that you would be biting everyone's head off everyday. If this were happening to me, I'd have decked someone by now." I knew he was right, and I held him tightly. I wanted to cry, but I couldn't. I was afraid that if I started crying, I wouldn't be able to stop. I couldn't sleep that night. My chest just kept burning as I relived in my head everything that was happening, looking for some kind of magical answer. The only thing that came to mind was what my mom taught me: drink milk for heartburn. So, I got up and drank some milk.

The next day I reported Gray and King to IA. Our office Investigative Aid, Yolanda Rios, agreed to be a witness and spoke to the IA agent over the speakerphone with Ruben and I. I was very proud of Yolanda for being honest and having a spine to take a stand with us. We all knew that she would face retaliation for this. Her coming forward took a lot of guts.

On February 16, 1999, I got my usual midnight warning phone call from Sector (Customs National Dispatch Center), advising me that I had to be in Thermal, at the airport at 0600hrs for a load (controlled delivery of narcotics) from Calexico. When I hung up the phone, I was half asleep and wondered if the call was real or if I had just dreamt it again. I remembered how a couple of years ago I dreamt of a load call, got up, did my usual getting ready in 15 minutes, jumped in my car and left. As I was attempting to come up on the radio to ascertain where I was supposed to be, Sector seemed confused. After much checking, and a call to my boss over the radio, I realized that I had dreamt the call.

I remember how the next morning when I walked into the office, Allen Casey came over the intercom, in a radio voice, "Ah Sector, Sector, where am I supposed to be, Sector? 915, 915, (my call sign) you're dreaming, 915. Click your heals three times and then you can go home." As I walked down the hall in total humiliation, Ruben and Jerry walked past me with their arms up, like they were sleepwalking, giggling. Of course my mature response was to attempt not to grin and to curse them under my breath. Later that morning Bob Mattivi came over the intercom and said, "Everyone involved in tomorrow's escapades please retire to the back for the briefing. Oh, and Earth to Darlene, Earth to Darlene, Darlene, wake up. This is a real message." My follow-up response was to get on the intercom and say, "Uh, Bob, up yours." When I walked to the back, everyone was pretending to be asleep and snoring.

Well, unfortunately, this time it was real. Once again, they were waking everyone up at midnight to give them a heads-up for a load at 0600hrs. I thought to myself, "Why do they do this? Why don't they just let us sleep until about 0500hrs and then wake us up?" It is always so hard for me to get back to sleep. Still, it was going to be nice to see the boys from Calexico. As much as Evantie had tried to undermine relationships between RAIC/Riverside and Calexico, to make Ricardo look bad, some of us saw right through him.

The load came in late, as usual, at about noon. It was hot in Thermal, 115 degrees, and I had little sleep. When the boys from the Calexico office pulled up, Carlos Osorio was with them. Carlos was a great agent, a Latino, a member of the ACEC, and my friend. He walked over and gave me a big bear hug. I glanced at Dave Gray, and he had a condescending look on his face. I wanted so badly to walk over, curl my little fist up and knock that smirk off of his face. "What a bigot," I thought.

The load ended up in a bad part of L.A., where they always seemed to end up. We had to hook up with the SAIC/LA guys. By this time, Ruben, Carlos and I were looked upon with fear and disgust because of our whistleblowing. The L.A. guys treated us like they were afraid to be seen talking to us, like we had the plague. Some of these guys I had known for years and had sat with for hours on details and had gone through some dicey situations with. Now, none of them would even make eye contact with me. I concealed my hurt at their betrayal by making my usual bad jokes.

We briefed up, and not surprisingly, out of 13 guys, Carlos, Ruben and I, were on the entry team. I'm sure the L.A. guys saw us as expendable. Carlos was first to do the knock and notice, supposedly because of his Spanish skills. It was funny how that worked out, we had a uniformed LAPD officer with us, who also spoke Spanish, but Carlos was still lead-in. I was next and then Ruben. I stood there remembering the "Surviving Armed Confrontation Course" that we had recently completed. I remembered them saying that the most dangerous part of an entry was the second and third position of the entry team. When the first guy enters, often times the crooks don't have time to react, but the second and third person are like sitting ducks in the doorway, no matter how fast you're moving. I said to Ruben and Carlos, "Is this the big hint, or what?" I thought, "Well, Carlos is so big, I'll just tuck in behind him, hold on to his shirt, and hope for the best."

By this time it was 2000hrs. The crooks took a long time getting from Thermal to L.A. "Don't they know how tired I am?" I asked Ruben. He responded, "I see you got the midnight heads-up call, too. Why doesn't someone have sense enough to call us the next morning? Why wake us up twice?" "My thoughts exactly," I said. Carlos subtly pulled Ruben and I aside and quietly said, "Nice entry team they put together here, huh? Notice how the case agent can't seem to ascertain whether or not this house has any firearms registered, a real no-brainer for the rest of us. Look, we go in fast and low. I'll go right, Dar left, Ruben straight. Remember, low and fast. I don't like the looks of this at all." I thought, "Well, there goes my human barricade."

We went in fast and hard. I went left into the kitchen where I found two toddlers in highchairs at the table. I came around the doorway with my gun drawn, and the toddlers screamed. I lowered my gun and quickly holstered it. I then tried to quiet the toddlers. "This always makes me feel terrible. I scared these little kids to death, and now I have to calm them down." I noticed that they were in there alone, strapped to their chairs. It seemed as though they had been there for a while. The Cheerios on their highchair tables were stale, and their diapers were smelly, obviously soiled.

Carlos gave the "all clear" signal. I unstrapped the kids and took them to the living room, holding and comforting them. I gave one of them my badge and the other my keys to play with. I asked one of the L.A. guys where the mom was and he answered, "She's probably one of the crack-heads blown out in here (pointing toward the bedroom) with the others; typical Mexicans." I looked over at the staircase and saw Ruben standing at the top. Unbeknownst to the L.A. guy, Ruben heard this comment. I saw the pain on his face. When he saw me reading him, he looked embarrassed, turned his head, paused and walked back up the stairs. I thought of how many times in the past year I had seen this pain, not only on Ruben, but on my Latino husband as well. Part of me wanted to head-butt the L.A. agent with a shotgun, and part of me wanted to run after Ruben and console him, but all I did was find some Pampers, change the toddlers, and remind myself that we made it through the door alive, and that was worth something.

This little escapade gave Ruben, Carlos and I a chance to talk. We explained to Carlos more about what we were doing in organizing the ACEC (Association of Customs Employees for Change). He was very supportive, but I still saw fear, even in a big, tough-guy bruiser like

Carlos. When the toughest people around you are afraid, the world can be a pretty insecure place with nowhere to run and hide.

I got home late that night because the search warrant and suspect booking took forever. I had been up for over 24 hours now. I was just in time to chug some more coffee, have breakfast with my kids and go back to work. My little Ian said, "Mom, I missed you at breakfast and when I came home from school yesterday. I said, "I missed you too handsome, but I'm here now. Can I eat with you?" Sarah and Ian responded with great big hugs. I was so tired, and for a split second I thought of going upstairs and grabbing a few winks, but I had breakfast with my kids instead. I worried about how this job was affecting my role as a parent, and then I reminded myself of the fact that my kids were never strapped to a highchair for hours with soiled diapers and stale Cheerios while I smoked crack in the next room. Once again, I was making a weak attempt at justifying my job.

I arrived at the office about 0900hrs. As I was pulling into the parking lot, Ruben was getting out of his car. Both of us were getting 911 pages from Sandy. Ruben saw me looking at my pager and said, "You, too? That Sandy and her 911 pages! You know I love her to death, but you just never know if it is a real 911, or if it is just some juicy info." "I know," I said. "I told her to stop doing that and she just doesn't listen."

Ruben and I did a three-way call to Sandy, and she was crying. She told us that she and Shannon Getz were going to be interviewed today by IA, and it had something to do with Huge World. Huge World was a technology network-marketing group that Sandy, Ervin Rios and I had all joined. For a nominal entry fee, you became a distributor and got technology products at a reduced rate. It kind of worked like Avon, but for technology. I was interested in the Internet course they offered. None of us had any intention of selling any of these products; we only wanted to get the products and training that was offered at some really decent rates.

I instructed her to take a tape recorder and a witness. She told me that she didn't have one. I told her to stop what she was doing right now, and go and get one. She assured me that she would. When Ruben and I hung up, I again saw pain on his face. Ruben said, "Those jerks, they are never going to stop, are they, Darlene?" As much as Ruben liked to moan and complain about how Sandy and I drove him crazy, I knew that Ruben cared deeply about us and what was happening to us. I knew he somehow felt a sense of responsibility for what was happening to us, and it wore on him. I tried a lame attempt at "bucking us both up." "Ruben, Sandy's tough. When she gets through crying she'll be ticked off, and she'll handle this like the pro that she is. She's tough, Ruben. She can handle this," I said.

Sandy called me later that day and gave me the scoop. She sounded much better. She sounded like the brave fighter I knew her to be, and I was relieved. She had gotten a tape recorder and recorded the session. Sure enough, IA was grilling her about Huge World.

I couldn't believe that this is what IA was going to hang their hat on. I briefed Ruben over lunch and more Mountain Dews. At 1500hrs, I had been awake for 36 hours straight. I had had so much Mountain Dew that my hands were shaking. I thought to myself, "Mountain Dew should do a commercial with Federal Narcotics Agents on how we all use it to stay awake on the job." I wasn't sure if I was shaking from the Dew, over what happened to Sandy, or the lack of sleep. It was probably a combination of them all. I went to the gym to relieve my stress. I swam the mile in 52 minutes. I made a mental note to try getting angry and drinking a ton of Mountain Dew right before the Police Olympics.

On March 10, 1999, SA Janet Somers informed Ruben that Easel had admitted to her, as well as SA Scott Chandler of the SAIC/LA office and AUSA Bailey Miller in September 1998, that Easel did in fact take the heroin evidence home. That would be instrumental in our proof that there is selective enforcement of regulations on agents and that enforcement of agency policy is used only on whistleblowers, not the "good old boys." Ruben contacted me at the U.S. Attorneys office to tell me this news. I was there picking up subpoenas, one of which I would have to serve in Calexico. I told Ruben that he needed to go with me to serve this subpoena and that this would give us a perfect opportunity to brief Ricardo Sandoval, the RAIC/Calexico, about the upcoming ACEC (Association of Customs Employees for Change) meeting.

Chapter Nineteen

Trip to Calexico

When I got back to the office I signed out for the next day in order to go to Calexico with Ruben to serve subpoenas. In the federal agent world, serving subpoenas is a routine, normal course of business. We simply sign out where we are going to be, and no one ever asks any questions. As soon as Evantie saw that Ruben and I were going to go to Calexico, he came into my office and approached me at my desk. He asked, "Uh, hey Dar, what's this you're going to Calexico for?" I showed him the subpoena. He looked at me with an expression of confusion and said, "So, you have to go to Calexico then? Can't you just mail this or something?" I thought to myself, "What a dunce. Where did he get his training from, Wal-Mart School of Investigators?" Everyone knows (anyone that has ever completed a successful criminal case, that is) that these federal criminal subpoenas have to be served in person. I responded suspiciously, "Yes, Boss, it has been a standing requirement from the U.S. Attorney's office for years now that these have to be delivered in person." Evantie said, "Oh, OK, just wondering what was going on."

Evantie went back to his office, and less than a minute later, he returned. I was on the phone, and he stood there looking at me impatiently. He was clearly indignant that I didn't immediately hang up on the caller and jump to attention. Evantie sighed and made a twirling finger gesture to me, indicting that I needed to hang up and give him my attention.

I hung up the phone and said, "What do you need, Boss?" Evantie asked, "Why do you need to take Ruben with you?" Again I thought,

125

"Where is this guy's brain!" I said condescendingly, "Evantie, it's stan-
dard agency policy that due to officer safety concerns, no agent will
serve a subpoena alone." Evantie replied, "I know that, but why are you
taking Ruben?" I answered his obviously paranoid question with a
question, "Why not Ruben? I mean, is there some kind of problem here,
sir? Are agents now being told whom they can or can't take with them to
serve a subpoena? I've worked here 11 years now, and no one has ever
questioned me or anyone else as to the selection of agents to serve sub-
poenas." I knew what Evantie was up to. He was going to try to keep
Ruben and me from having contact with Ricardo Sandoval. He knew we
would make good use of our time, and this just killed him. Evantie,
fumbling for an answer, said, "Well, I was just concerned about whether
Ruben was available or not." "Sir," I said, "I wouldn't have put him on
the sign out board if I hadn't already cleared it with him."

He stood there trying to cleverly disguise his agenda with feigned
concern, desperately trying to come up with his next genius idea of why
Ruben and I couldn't go to Calexico. Naturally, I was disgusted!   I
looked at him, shook my head, reached for the phone, started dialing,
and said, "You know what, Evantie, why don't I call the AUSA Yvette and
let you explain your concerns to her of how you don't want me to do my
job on this case. I'd really like to hear your explanation to a federal pros-
ecutor of why her subpoena isn't going to be served." Evantie said in a
spineless tone, "No, no, that's all right, I just don't understand why you
have to take Ruben with you." I shot back, "And you still haven't given
me justification as to why *not* Ruben!" Evantie sighed in exasperation
and walked away.

On March 11, 1999, Ruben came to my house to pick me up for our
trip to Calexico. Our original game plan was to ride together. After
Ruben arrived, we thought it better to drive both vehicles to the I-10
freeway split at the Beaumont exit. We would then leave one vehicle
there and carpool to Calexico. This would save Ruben from having to
bring me back to my house at the end of the day. Ruben walked out of

my house first to go to his vehicle. I got to the doorway and went back in to turn off the TV. Ruben was already in his car, had turned around and headed up the street when I came out. As I walked to my car door, I observed a surveillance vehicle watching us. The vehicle started down the street straight towards my house, and the driver, upon spotting me, ducked into a parking space. It was very obvious that the driver was startled to see me. I stood next to my car, turned towards this strange vehicle and stared at it. The driver pulled a fast U-turn and sped off.

As if this bonehead maneuver wasn't obvious enough, when I got into my car and started to catch up with Ruben, there was another strange vehicle parked on the next block. As I drove past it I slowed down and maneuvered my vehicle over to the opposite side of the street to get close to the strange vehicle. Someone on the driver's side was attempting to duck down and hide. I then heard several long squelch sounds come over my radio. I had learned from several sources, one of which was David Gray, Mr. IA himself, that when IA is conducting a surveillance on their secret stealth channel, their radio transmissions come over our radios as squelch. I wanted to alert Ruben on the radio, but I knew IA would be listening. I floored it to catch up with Ruben. I caught up with him a few blocks away, and lit him up (turned my police lights on). He saw me and waited at the traffic light. I jumped out of my car, ran up to him at the intersection and quickly explained what I had just seen.

We drove to the freeway and parked my car in the Denny's parking lot. I jumped in with Ruben, and we began to conduct counter-surveillance to lose our tail. Ruben thought I had probably startled them when they first came around the corner and saw me at my car. I wasn't supposed to be there. They obviously thought I would be leaving in Ruben's car and didn't count on our leaving in separate vehicles. When they saw Ruben leave, they thought that I was with him and were trying to catch up to Ruben's vehicle when I came out of my house.

We saw several more really brilliant stunts and burned (slang term for identifying a surveillance) the IA surveillance to the ground. Ruben, being the clever, street savvy agent that he was, lost the IA stooges lickety-split. Ruben and I couldn't believe how stupid and obvious they had been. I was convinced that before Customs issued their IA decoder ring, they gave each IA agent a frontal lobotomy.

It took us about three hours to get to Calexico. When we arrived, Ricardo was very happy to see us. He greeted us with warmth and professional hospitality. His office was unlike any government supervisor's office I had ever seen. He had a beautiful portrait of Dr. Martin Luther King, Jr., as well as the Mexican flag, hanging in his office. He didn't have the normal narcissistic cop memorabilia hanging all over the walls. It looked very classy and professional. We talked for a while and then he invited us to lunch. As we walked to his car, a vehicle passed us in the parking lot. Ricardo told us that it was an IA vehicle. He'd seen it all too many times. We sat in his vehicle for a while talking, and the same vehicle passed us, circling in the parking lot at least three times. Ricardo said, "Can you believe this?! These morons have nothing better to do but to nose around us." We told him about how we were surveilled from the house, and he was not surprised. Ricardo said laughingly, "Welcome to the club, guys. Now you know what my life has been like for a couple of years now. They follow me to work; they follow me home. My life is no longer my own. I have no privacy." As he spoke I could hear the pain and anguish in his voice. His face was a road map of suffering as his tired eyes watched IA pass by us again.

We drove to a nearby restaurant and sat in a booth by the window. The IA vehicle had followed us there, passing by several times. Ricardo explained in great detail about how when he became a whistleblower several years before and filed his lawsuit, his life was literally ripped from his grasp. He told us one story after another of the consistent and ongoing retaliation he had received at the hands of Internal Affairs. The fact that he used to be one of them (an IA investigator) did not matter.

He came under one bogus IA investigation after another, always being cleared in the end. He was currently under the 22nd investigation. I listened as he told us that this had almost destroyed his family life, and how he, too, had started using working out as a tool to relieve stress. Everyday after work he would go to the gym to lift weights. As he spoke, I noticed how fit he was. I wondered how many hours and how much work it must have taken to get to that degree of fitness. As I listened, I watched Ruben's face reflect the same pain and anguish. My heart ached for Ricardo.

One of the most appalling stories Ricardo told was about the "Mexican parking lot." Before Brinkley became the Director for the Office of Investigations, he was the ASAIC/San Diego. Brinkley and several other managers had what they called the "Mexican parking lot." This was where all Latinos had to park their old, beat-up G-rides. Latinos were never issued good cars, and Brinkley made them park in a lot away from the office so as not to embarrass the SAIC office. Ricardo worked at the SAIC/San Diego at the time and received this same treatment. I explained to Ricardo that this was exactly what was happening to Ruben at our RAIC office.

This all just sickened me. My hatred for Brinkley and others like him was growing darker and deeper. I couldn't help but think of all the times my poor husband, also Latino, tried to point out the obvious discrimination to me, but I just didn't see it. I would always tell him that he was just seeing things, that he was paranoid. How I wished I could take those words back. I wished that I had listened to him and offered some support and consolation. White or not, I would never see things through white Anglo eyes again.

As I drove home from Denny's that night, I felt like every car was watching me. It was like I had been stripped naked in a crowd of strangers. I felt paranoid, violated, frustrated and angry. I thought of how this daily stress for over two years now must have worn Ricardo down. No amount of money from a lawsuit and no promotion could ever make up for this. They had taken away this man's life, and I saw first hand what that had done to him. I don't know how he had kept it together for so long. I hadn't endured half of the abuse he had received, and already it was all I could do to keep from running over Evantie and Brinkley in a parking lot. I worried that I wouldn't have the courage or stamina to go the distance Ricardo had. My mind raced with anguish, fear and anger. I almost had a wreck on the freeway because of my inattentive driving.

On March 29, 1999, I sent an affidavit and formal complaint by certified mail to the Director of the Regional EEO Complaint Center regarding the role SAIC/LA and RAIC/Riverside management played in the refusal of the Postal Inspectors to lift a finger to investigate the crimes committed against me (i.e. the threatening letter and phony transcript). On April 2, 1999, I received a response at my home from the Regional Complaint Center regarding this issue. This response had a March 30, 1999 date stamp, and had been signed by Luanne Holmes, Director. In this response, Ms. Holmes dismissed my formal complaint, stating that it is not within the purview of the EEO regulations. I wondered, "How in the world could my formal complaint be dismissed on March 30th, when it had only been received at the Regional Complaint Center on April 1, 1999, the date verified by certified mail return receipt?" Subsequently, I wrote a letter to Ms. Holmes and sent copies of the certified mail returned receipt, asking her where it was that she obtained an ability to know the contents of a complaint, and turn it down, before she even received it. I never got a response.

Chapter Twenty

ACEC

On April 5, 1999, I attended a meeting of the Association of Customs Employees for Change (ACEC) at the Mission Inn in Riverside, California. Sandy Nunn, Ervin Rios, Ruben Sandoval, Rick Sandoval, Marissa New and Justine Pierce, who was the second in command for EEO at the Customs headquarters level, were present. The purpose of the meeting was to establish a united front and an organization (ACEC) to fight the cronyism and corruption we had all encountered. We presented plenty of evidence to prove our point to Justin Pierce. He assured us that he would be a facilitator between the Customs Commissioner and us. Ruben wanted to trust him, but I was still very leery. I told Ruben that it didn't matter if this guy was honorable or not, if he pushed the wrong buttons, and didn't actively participate in shutting us down, Pierce would just become one of us. The Commissioner would simply kill his own messenger, figuratively speaking.

At this meeting, I read to the group a letter written by Sandy. It was a professional, yet scathing letter reporting much of the corruption, cronyism and retaliation that we had witnessed. With Sandy, the pen really is mightier than the sword. This letter had a petition-style attachment that contained the signatures of 26 Customs employees (including inspectors, agents, supervisors, intelligence analyst, etc). It had been sent the day prior to this meeting to numerous senators and congressmen, particularly in our state of California, as well as Customs Commissioner Ray Kelly and Customs Commissioner of Internal Affairs Harrison Wells. As I read the letter aloud, I could see Pierce squirming in his chair. He was not pleased, but I clearly was. He gave me a look as if to say, "You've gone too far." I glared back at him intensely as I read, as if to say, "I've only just begun." As I read, every emotion that I'd been feeling over the past few months was aching to come to the surface. I grit my teeth and choked down my anger. My face felt hot and I thought I was going to have a stroke trying to maintain control and dignity. When I finished, I looked up at the faces of everyone in the room and could see the same road map of emotional distress. I then looked at Pierce who was also observing the emotion of the room, and on his face I saw fear and hopelessness. I knew then that not only would he not help us, but even if he wanted to, he knew it was futile. My anger dissolved into hopelessness, and I remained quiet for the remainder of the meeting.

During a break, Ricardo gave me a copy of a statement by Robert Saitley. Saitley was an ASAIC under SAIC/LA, Drake Brinkley. He had been running the largest undercover money laundering operation ever conducted by any agency in U.S. history, Operation Casablanca. Saitley read a statement before the House of Representatives Subcommittee on Criminal Justice, Drug Policy and Human Resources. The following are excerpts from this statement.

> Beginning in the fall of 1997, Mr. Drake Brinkley leaked information about Operation Casablanca. At a law enforcement conference in Tampa, Florida, Mr. Brinkley provided information about this undercover operation to a network news executive.
>
> Later in the investigation, Mr. Brinkley invited several congressional staff representatives to Los Angeles to be briefed on a major undercover money laundering investigation. Upon their arrival he not only paraded them through the undercover offsite, which housed the Alpha Task Force, he took them to the audio and video

monitoring station of the undercover storefront, "Golden Empire."

During my meeting with the Commissioner of Customs, I requested an official document which reports the findings of the Internal Affairs investigation related to Mr. Brinkley's false and malicious accusation. To this day, I have received no official response from any Customs Service Officer in regard to any of the topics I discussed with the Commissioner.

As I read Robert Saitly's statement I thought, "Poor man!" Now Saitly is going to have the IA goon squad after him just like the rest of us whistleblowers. I didn't know him that well, but the general consensus was that he was an honorable and direct man and an excellent manager. I was familiar with some of his casework, and I found him to be both impressive and professional. Saitly was definitely experienced, which was more than anyone could ever say about Brinkley. I remarked to Ricardo how hypocritical this whole system was: I received a letter of disciplinary action for allegedly releasing confidential information in submitting letters of commendation to EEO, but Brinkley exposes an undercover investigation and two undercover sites endangering the lives of undercover agents and confidential sources, and he walks away clean. Where is IA when it comes to the Customs "Mafia" managers?

I continued on with Ricardo, "You just watch; magically, Robert Saitly will come under some sort of bogus IA investigation." Ricardo responded, "He already has Dar, he already has." Just then it hit me: Operation Casablanca was targeting the infamous Arellano-Felix narcotics smuggling cartel. My tanker car seizure and subsequent investigation was targeting the same organization. I had information verifying that the dope I had seized was in fact Arellano-Felix dope. My head started spinning. Here Brinkley had made it his personal vendetta to undermine not only my criminal case, but he torpedoed the entire rail project as well. Simultaneously, Brinkley was torpedoing Saitly's multi-million dollar undercover money laundering projects as well. As I put two and two together, a rush of adrenalin hit me like a brick.

As soon as the ACEC meeting was over, I told Ruben I had to split. He and the others wanted me to stay and strategize some more, but I told them I had to get back to the office. Ruben sensed that something was up and asked, "Wow, Dar, what's going on?" I looked at him and said, "I'm not sure yet, but I feel like this house of cards may be a comin' down." I went back to the office and plowed into the Customs automated systems of importations. I began pulling entries of cars I had looked at. At the beginning of my rail project I had put what's called a "general hold" for weight on all pressurized tanker cars coming into the U.S. This meant that no car should have been cleared by any Customs officer without the car first being directed to one of the two rail yards that can do this: Texas and Colton, California. I immediately found several releases that were not authorized. I wasn't as familiar with this portion of the Customs computer system as it had been designed primarily for inspectors, so I immediately got a hold of Ervin Rios and asked him to meet me.

Chapter Twenty-one

The Pieces Fit

Ervin was about to pull his shift at UPS and we agreed to meet at his office. When I walked in, he knew something was up. I bluntly asked, "Who has the authority to release a general hold placed by O.I. (Customs' term for Office of Investigations—the Agents chain of command)?" Ervin answered, "Only a supervisor with subsequent notification to the agent." "Ervin, are you sure about that?" I asked. He leaned toward me with rising curiosity and said, "Why, Dar? What's going on? Whatcha got?" I took the entries from inside the jacket I was wearing, but just as I was bringing them out to show him, his supervisor walked in. I quickly put them back in my jacket. I felt my heart pounding and my head racing. We made small talk with the supervisor, told him some lame story to explain what I was doing there, and then he left.

I pulled out the entries again and showed him what I had found. He explained to me that there was a space on the entry where the supervisor releasing the general hold, by regulation, was supposed to put in his four-digit code. I remembered that on the last three tanker cars we were trying to look at, they had been released three times. Each time, I had to get the railroad to chase them down and send them back from central California to be weighed. Every railcar has a distinct eight or nine-digit code for tracking, identification, and billing/invoicing purposes, so I asked Ervin to pull up the car numbers. Sure enough, Customs personnel, not a blunder by the railroad as I had previously thought, had released these cars. I showed Ervin the statement of

Robert Saitly, and he quickly put the pieces together. Ervin's eyes got big—he seemed very excited.

Ervin went to his desk and unlocked a drawer. He pulled out a file that he had been maintaining very carefully. As he pulled it out, he looked out the glass window to make sure no one was coming. He showed me a hand written flowchart that he had created. It all stemmed from a cocaine seizure he had made at the airport involving a juvenile and a private jet that had been cleared from a Colombian private airline. Ervin's flow chart tracked the Arellano-Felix Cartel to two private aircraft that were conveniently owned by Mexican and Columbian banks. These banks were profiled in Robert Saitly's Casablanca Investigation, the undercover money laundering operation. Ervin also tracked the pilot of the aircraft from which he had seized the cocaine, to a company in Sineloa, Mexico. The name of this company was Grassa, the same name on the entry documents for the tanker carload of Arellano-Felix dope that I seized almost a year ago. Ervin said, "You know, Dar, when I seized the coke from this kid, my supervisor was all over me. He was outraged and tried to undermine me, all at the direction of the Port Director, Wyndal Nabrowski.

"There's more," Ervin said. "There's an ex-inspector with whom I have spoken; his name is Jeff Weitzman." When Ervin said his name, it rang a bell with me. Ervin continued, "His name rings a bell because he was the inspector who nailed the famous 'Hydro' truck tanker load of cocaine at the Otay Mesa port of entry. "Oh, yeah, I remember," I said. "Well," Ervin continued, "when Weitzman profiled this car, he put a hold on it in ACS for secondary, the location that inspectors move vehicles to for inspection/entry. Someone released the hold without authorization, and it was just coincidence that Weitzman was working the line and happened to see it coming. He secondaried it anyway, and just as he was about to run his dog on it, his supervisor ordered him to release it. Well, he ran the dog anyway, and the dog went crazy. Weitzman defied the orders of his supervisor and popped it open to find one of the biggest seizures of cocaine ever. When Weitzman confronted his supervisor about who ordered the car released, the supervisor said it was by order of the Port Director, Adrian Garcia."

I sat back in my chair and shook my head. It was common knowledge throughout the agency that Adrian Garcia had been under one corruption investigation after another by the FBI. He was infamous for rumors about a connection with the Arellano-Felix Cartel. Ervin then pulled out a picture from his file. It was a picture of Adrian Garvacio, Customs uniform on, with his arm around Carlos Ray Horn, infamous leader of a Mexican smuggling cartel that works with the Arellano-Felix Organization. "You've got to be kidding me!" I exclaimed. "Ervin, did you know that Adrian Garcia and Brinkley go way back?" Ervin said that he had heard that, but wasn't sure. I added that I had also heard that Ervin's prior Port Director, Wyndal Nabrowski, was tight with both Garcia and Brinkley. These people all came up together within Customs. Brinkley had worked the southern border on and off for about 30 years.

Then Ervin rolled his chair even closer to me, and in almost a whisper he said, "Dar, do you remember back in the late 1980's and through the early 1990's hearing about the 'Blue Ribbon Commission Investigation' initiated by Congress?" "Yeah," I responded. "As a matter of fact, I remember it very well. At that time, I was assigned to the Personal Protection Detail of the Commissioner of Customs every time she came to L.A. She spoke quite often of this investigation and having to respond to Congress." Ervin said, "Well, I have the entire two thousand-and-something page transcript of those proceedings; and you know what? The same people that we're dealing with, Brinkley, Nabrowski, and Mr. IA himself, Harrison Wells, all their names are all over that investigation. There was a female OIG investigator named Cherry Rollins and an attorney/private investigator by the name of Jason Fielding assigned to the Congressional Investigation. Cherry Rollins resigned from the OIG in disgust because of all of the stonewalling she had received from Customs in her efforts to conduct her investigation. Jason Fielding was found in his driveway in Long Beach: two to the chest and one to the head. It was ruled a botched burglary attempt—I'm not buying it. Who else shoots like that? Only cops. This poor man was executed in his driveway in front of his little daughter. No doubt he stumbled onto something just like we did."

Ervin then stated, "Dar, think of the timing of when I got fired; think of what we were doing." Just then it hit me, and I said, "Oh my gosh! That was right after we did the first tanker car, and we started working in the rail yard." "That's right!" Ervin said. "My supervisor was giving me hell every step of the way. He didn't want me working on the rail project with you at all. Darlene, this isn't a coincidence! They don't want us working these railcars for a reason. We're not supposed to be over there! And doesn't it kind of make you wonder about your 'Geraldo Rivera' tanker car? Maybe it wasn't so empty after all!"

My mind was racing. I began to recall how we were all so sure that there was no way anyone could have unloaded that tanker car during the trip up from Calexico in the time frame that it was unaccounted for. At the time, we were all so sure that the only way that they could have opened that car and removed the contents was via a specialized facility, like the one in Colton. The commodity contained in the car at that time was some sort of fuel. Then I thought of how easy it was for the crooks on this last loaded car to simply "jury-rig" a tri-pod on top of the hatch and use a simple pulley and chain device hooked up to two fork lifts and poof, the hatch was opened! What we had originally thought to be almost impossible became plausible. The lost "Geraldo Rivera" car was missing for approximately nine to twelve hours. This would have been enough time for the crooks to track the car off onto a small spur somewhere between Calexico and Colton, and then access the load. Based upon what happened to this last loaded car on the controlled delivery, this wasn't out of the realm of possibility anymore. In fact, when you're talking about the kind of money we're dealing with, millions of dollars in narcotics, it is well within the realm of possibility. As I tried to comprehend all of this, I sat back in my chair in total disillusion, feeling like a fool who had just realized how bad he'd been had. I recalled defending my agency to the media. The media had been making the accusation that the empty tanker car, the "Geraldo Rivera" car, was in fact loaded, and that during the time frame that it was unaccounted for, the crooks off-loaded it.

Had they been right? Had I foolishly assumed the best of my agency and failed to dig into these accusations because of my inexperience and naive loyalty to my agency? Ervin saw me sitting there staring blankly and waved his hand back and forth in front of my face saying, "Earth to Darlene, Earth to Darlene, come in please." He got my attention and said, "Dar, I'm thinking that you're thinking that the 'Geraldo Rivera' car was loaded, and the crooks got to the stuff just like they did this last one, with a tri-pod and everything. That *is* what you're thinking, isn't it?" I looked at him with an "Oh man, I really messed up" look on my face, and nodded, "yes." Ervin said, "Dar, if we're right and they killed that private investigator, Jason, because he found something, just imagine what they would do to cover up the kind of stuff we've found. Maybe he found out the same things. If they've killed once, it won't bother them to kill again. I mean, look what they've already done, and they don't even know what we've discovered about this railcar business. Think about it Dar, if we're right, this is a billion-dollar thing we're attempting to disrupt, and people have been killed for a whole lot less."

We both sat there in disbelief. I asked, "Who else have you shown this stuff to?" "No one," he replied. "Good," I said, "don't." I picked up the phone and called AUSA Yvette Palazuelos. I told her that Ervin and I needed to meet with her, and couldn't discuss it over the phone. She agreed. When I got off of the phone, Ervin and I looked at each other and began to laugh nervously. I told Ervin, "I hope this place ain't bugged, or else we're toast. Look, do you have any contacts at LAPD so we could pull the files on the Jason Fielding murder investigation?"

Ervin responded with a confident smile, "You know me, Dar. I have contacts everywhere." When I left there, for the first time I was riddled with fear, and my anger had taken a back seat. I thought of that poor private investigator being executed in front of his little girl. I was convinced that this wasn't just a robbery. He had found out something he wasn't supposed to know, just like we had. I thought of my kids and my husband, and I was really worried. I was now convinced that my dream really was a warning. These must be some sort of guardian angels sent to give me a message, and the message was coming through loud and clear, "GET OUT!"

On April 21, 1999, I got a call from Sandy Nunn. She told me that Robert Saitly just walked into the SAIC/LA office, turned in his badge and gun, and retired before his minimum mandatory retirement. I couldn't believe it. Saitly was one of the toughest men in Customs, and he just threw in the towel and walked away. I began to seriously consider my options and listen to my head, and not my ego.

Later that day, Ricardo called me. He told me about Cynthia Stone, a woman who used to work for him in IA and was still a good friend of his. Cynthia's husband was a DEA agent. About a year or so ago, Cynthia had to attend some IA training at FLETC (Federal Law Enforcement Training Center) with David Gray. This was while Gray was still in IA before he came to the RAIC/Riverside office. Ricardo said that she wanted to talk to me about something, and that he'd call me at home tonight; he didn't trust the phones. Later that night I got a call from Ricardo at home. He told me that while Cynthia Stone and David Gray were at the school, they went to the "queer bar" (cop slang for the small bar located just outside the gates of FLETC) together one night. Cynthia had a few too many drinks, and Gray acted like a gentleman and offered to walk her back to her dorm. When they got to her dorm, Gray attempted to force himself on her. Ricardo said it was all she could do to beat him off. She screamed as loud as she could, and he got scared and left.

The next day, Sandy and I called Cynthia. She told us that the reason she didn't come forward soon after it happened was that she was afraid of Gray and the power he had with IA. She knew full well how IA was used within the agency. But now that she no longer worked for Customs, she was willing to come forward. I assured her that I would relay this information to the appropriate agency. When I got off of the phone with Cynthia and Sandy, I thought to myself, "What am I, the whistleblower hotline?" I knew that Gray already resented me. Now he would hate me for sure. I documented my conversation with Cynthia, and Ruben and I reported it to both the Treasury Inspector General's Office and the FBI.

April 23, 1999, Ervin Rios and I met with AUSA Yvette. Before we went into her office, Ervin met me outside and explained to me that the homicide investigation files of Jason Fielding had magically disappeared and that his contacts at LAPD were at a loss as to why they couldn't find them. Then he reminded me that our beloved Port Director, Wyndal Nabrowski, used to work for LAPD and often bragged about all his contacts there. "This is no coincidence, Dar," Ervin said. "This is no coincidence. These files aren't misplaced or lost. These files are buried!" He also told me that several Inspector friends of his had told him that Senator Fienstein was seen a couple of days ago on the Customs yacht with Drake Brinkley. This was just a few weeks after Sandy's letter (the letter signed by Customs employees alleging corruption) was sent to senators and congressmen, including Senator Fienstein, via certified mail. All of the pieces were coming together like a dark, abstract jigsaw puzzle. I wondered just how far up the chain corruption went. My fear grew.

We went into Yvette's office and explained to her what we had put together. I showed her the tanker car entries that had been released, as well as the picture of the Customs port director with Cartel leader Carlos Ray Horn and brought attention to his long-standing relationship with Drake Brinkley and Harrison Wells. We explained the connections between the Casablanca money laundering operation and the tanker car case and how they both involved the Arellano-Felix Cartel. We further explained our suspicions about Brinkley, Harrison Wells, and the rest—it was no coincidence that Brinkley was torpedoing Casablanca as well as the rail project. We also told her about the Congressional Blue Ribbon Commission Investigation into corruption in Customs some 10 years ago involving some of the same people, and of the murder of Jason Fielding, the private investigator/attorney who was conducting an investigation into the same people. We told her we were confident that all of this was not just coincidence. She listened carefully, seemed very concerned, and told us that she would brief the AUSA's on the Casablanca case.

Chapter Twenty-two

The Demonstration

A couple of nights later, Sandy called me to discuss the idea of a demonstration. She had gotten the idea from the demonstrations that were being held in downtown Riverside protesting the Riverside Police. The demonstrators believed that the shooting of a black girl, who had been allegedly asleep in her vehicle at the time, was racially motivated. As I thought about this, I realized just how much I had changed. Five years ago, I would have immediately defended the cops, not questioning their actions. I began to see the incidents with different eyes because of what had happened to me. I remembered the first time I saw the videotape of the Rodney King beating. I thought I saw what appeared to be law enforcement at its worst. I learned later that the mainstream media did not play the entire Rodney King tape, including the "lunge" King made toward an arresting officer's gun. But to me, it appeared that some of those cops were out of control. Yet the next day when I went to work, everyone in the office was defending the cops' actions, claiming it was part of their training. I thought to myself, "Well, maybe I missed something, or maybe they saw something that I didn't." At the time, I stayed clear of the King discussion because everyone was so emotional about it, but their seemingly blind defense of the police seemed only reflexive and never questioning. I didn't have the spine to stand up for my views, but I believed the entire matter was worthy of an objective review. I thought that if the cops did everything they were trained to do, what harm would come from an official inquiry? I would later realize that to be silent about these things is, in essence, blindly defending it when other facts might justify a different conclusion. I regretted my silence. I did not agree that law enforcement officers should stick together no matter what. I always believed that bad actions by some officers might require that other officers take actions against them, as much as that could be distressful. Loss of public trust in law enforcement was the greater issue.

Although Sandy's demonstration idea scared me and even seemed a bit drastic, I started thinking about something a reporter had once told me when he was trying to get me to go public. He said, "Sometimes the best protection you can get is only found when you come into the light." I thought of the regret I felt about not voicing my opinion regarding previous incidents. I didn't want to continue to be a coward and live with the regret. Nothing else had worked for us thus far. "So," I thought, "why not? This just might work."

We got our attorney, Tom Allison on a conference call and discussed the idea. Tom mentioned that he had just learned that the Customs Commissioner was scheduled to appear the following Monday in front of a congressional committee and announce how he has everything in Customs under control. Tom said, "Talk about timing! Just picture it: here he is bragging to Congress about how he has things under control, and then someone interrupts him and tells him that there are Customs Agents demonstrating in front of the RAIC/Riverside announcing a huge class action lawsuit for discrimination and retaliation against whistleblowers."

I expressed some concerns about trying to put a demonstration together on such short notice. Sandy assured me that we could do it, so we put in a call to Ruben. Much to my surprise, Ruben also thought it was a good idea. I was worried about how my husband might react to our going public, so I asked Ruben to talk to him. Ben was very supportive, but made it clear that he didn't want us discussing the tanker car corruption case. Ruben agreed that it was neither the time nor the place to expose our suspicions. We should only expose the retaliation against whistleblowers and the class action lawsuit.

After only a couple of days of burning up the phones and dealing with a logistical nightmare, we put together a nice little demonstration. We were treading a fine line between trying to keep this somewhat hush-hush because we didn't want management to find out and attempt to stop us, and telling enough people to get them to attend. I awarded Sandy Nunn the title "Networking Queen of the Universe" for all her amazing coordination of the event. We talked to Cathy Harris, the Atlanta whistleblower and author of "Flying While Black: A Whistleblower's Story." Harris is a Senior Customs Inspector who blew the whistle on Customs' policy of racial profiling black women at airports. Harris received the same retaliatory treatment as the rest of us and still showed the courage to fly in for the demonstration.

The Friday before the demonstration, both Ruben and I put in for annual leave for the following Monday. We were giggling like two school kids up to mischief as we filled out the leave sheets. I remember feeling a sense of empowerment about what we were doing. I felt brave and confident. How naive of us both.

Over the weekend Ruben, Tom Allison and I had a meeting at the Mission Inn Hotel. There we signed the paperwork to incorporate the ACEC and worked on our speeches. Monday morning all the key players met for breakfast at the Mission Inn. I finally got to meet, in person, the people I had been talking to on the phone for the past year or so: Mike Connor, Cathy Harris, Tom Allison, John Carman, and Stephen Young from Arizona. Tom gave each of us a copy of the press release he had prepared, and it read as follows:

> Today, the Association of Customs Employees (ACEC) and the Customs Employees Against Discrimination Association (CEADA) announce their joining of forces to seek a fundamental and important change in how the U.S. Customs Service treats its

employees. Tomorrow, the United States Senate will hold hearings on serious problems with Customs' Office of Internal Affairs. Some of these problems have come to light through the efforts of David Kidwell, a reporter for the Miami Herald, and present or former Customs employees who have suffered the denigration of the integrity of the Customs Service.

For too long, the Customs Office of Internal Affairs has been used by unscrupulous management officials to shield themselves and their associates from serious charges of wrongdoing. At the same time these same Customs officials have used Internal Affairs as a sword against those employees who dare challenge their misuse of authority. When employees raise legitimate concerns about management wrongdoing they are often ignored or subjected to retaliation. Employees who dare to file grievances, report wrongdoing, or claim discrimination are perceived to be disloyal to the agency, and thereafter wrongfully targeted for retaliation.

One of the most effective means available to retaliate against employees is the instigation of an Internal Affairs or administrative investigation against an employee. Internal Affairs and/or administrative investigations are undertaken against these employees for what are often petty, frivolous and false charges of wrongdoing. Subjecting Customs employees to unjustified investigation can, and does, ruin the careers of these employees. Unjustified investigation causes them and their families to suffer greatly.

How could these problems fester to the point that the public, many responsible government officials, including the Senate's Finance Committee, the Commissioner of Customs, and Customs employees themselves doubt the integrity of the Service? Because Internal Affairs, hiding under regulations and policies meant to protect legitimate investigations, is allowed to use the same regulations and policies to cover up their blunders and illegal actions. Customs' management reluctance to lift the veil of secrecy has led to the failure of the public trust. So long as the wrongdoers are able to escape public scrutiny for their actions, there will be abuses.

Today, the ACEC and CEADA call for an end to the discriminatory and retaliatory practices of the Customs Service, and those who have, and continue to use the Office of Internal Affairs to discriminate and retaliate against Customs employees. ACEC takes notice of, and hope from, the Commissioner of Customs' recent statement acknowledging the past abuses of Internal Affairs. However, we are here today to voice that retaliatory actions are still being undertaken against good and honest employees, and that the Commissioner's efforts to date have been unsuccessful. Unfortunately, the only means available to those who have been wronged is to band together and bring legal action against Customs. ACEC has therefore retained the Washington, D.C. law firm of Davis & Bentzen, P.L.L.C. to seek legal redress on behalf of its members. The firm may be contacted at 202-000-0000.

Tom's press release was elegant, dignified and perfectly fitting. As we read it, a feeling of "esprite de corps" (Latin for 'the spirit of the corps') came over the group, the likes of which I hadn't seen since I was in the military. We all felt as though we were well armed, ready to go into battle. I felt empowered and confident, and we could taste the justice that we had been hoping for for so long. This would be the last time any of us would have this feeling for a long time.

As we sat there eating breakfast together, I realized what a tremendous group of very experienced people we were going into battle with. We were all seasoned veterans who, prior to becoming whistleblowers, had immaculate careers and high profile cases. (Sandy had the famous "Jewelry Mart" case that had been previewed in *Newsweek* magazine; Mike Connor had several famous cases and had been interviewed on the TV news show "20/20"; Tom Allison was a previous supervisor for Customs with several record seizures before leaving Customs and obtaining his law degree; Shannon Getz was a prior FBI Agent and survivor of the Oklahoma City Bombing; Ervin Rios was a highly decorated Senior Customs Inspector; John Carmon and Cathy Harris were also highly decorated former Customs Inspectors, and Cathy was a soon to be published author; and Ruben and I have both had record seizures and high profile cases that were referred to in the media.)

Mike Connor gave us a bit of juicy information about our nemesis, Brinkley. He informed us that he and Brinkley had worked together for a while and had introduced Brinkley to his wife. The night that this introduction took place, Brinkley took his future wife (a civilian) bar-hopping in his G-ride. How ironic! Here Brinkley was trying to stick Ruben with 45 days on the bricks for having his kids in Ruben's G-ride, while Brinkley himself had been out joy riding with civilians on a bar-hopping excursion in *his* G-ride. Mike told us of how Stuart "Stew" Peters, ex-Internal Affairs investigator, had even better dirt on Brinkley involving an accidental discharge of his weapon that was covered up for Brinkley.

After breakfast, we all walked together from the Mission Inn to the RAIC/Riverside where we would take our stand. My husband, Ben, met us there with plenty of bottled water for everyone. He's a good man. Ruben's family and kids were also there. I thought about bringing my kids, but feared the negative consequences of having them exposed to the media. I've always distrusted the media. I viewed them as a bunch of sharks who cared little for accuracy and would sell their own mother for a story. I rarely gave a journalist the time of day, and even then, only gave information when it suited my needs, or management forced me to. How ironic, here I was now, putting my fate in the hands of the media.

I was selected as the MC for this thing. I introduced Cathy Harris, who proceeded to give a very charismatic speech addressing the abuse that she endured at the hands of the agency. I then introduced the local president of MAPA, the Mexican American Political Association. He, too, gave an excellent and supportive speech, stating that MAPA was going to file an official complaint with Congress on our behalf. Ruben was up next, and I was so proud to introduce him, and even more proud after his eloquent speech, that it just about brought me to tears. Lastly, Tom Allison read the press release he had written for us and then answered questions.

Overall, the demonstration went well and was organized and professional ... and we even had signs. I was, however, disappointed in the amount and quality of coverage given to us by the media. We were quoted in newspapers across the country, but all quotes were buried in small columns on the fourth or fifth page. Maybe this was pay-back for all of the arrogant, condescending remarks I had thrown their way in lieu of the information they sought on my cases.

Shannon Getz chose not to make any speeches but was interviewed by one of the reporters from the API News. I'll never forget what she said to this reporter because it put this whole experience into perspective for me. She told the reporter that in light of the tremendous amount of stress she experienced as a result of blowing the whistle, in comparison, becoming a whistleblower had been more traumatic than surviving the Oklahoma City bombing. As Shannon softly spoke these words in almost a whisper of a voice, the pain and fear she held inside began to show. She had tears in her eyes and her voice cracked. My heart was just torn up watching her.

My chest felt tight. I wanted so badly to hug her and show her compassion, but I could not. Her words brought on me a sense of fear, fear that if I went to her, I might somehow contract her weakness, like contracting an illness. I pretended not to hear her and made jokes with Ervin. From that day on, I found myself feeling uncomfortable around Shannon. I was afraid of becoming weak and beaten down like she was, much in the same way I sometimes feel uncomfortable around someone in a wheelchair—afraid that this could happen to me, too, but not if I keep my distance. I had developed a false sense of security believing that by distancing myself from others' weaknesses, it would somehow put up a magical force field, keeping me from their fate.

As I thought about this and how I was feeling toward Shannon and her weaknesses, I realized that what I was feeling, in a very real sense, was a sort of prejudice. Here I was, in the middle of a battle that was, in part, a battle to fight discrimination, and I was carrying deep inside me, a prejudice, a very real prejudice against the weak and helpless. I knew that this was born out of fear and learned early in my childhood. My fear of others' weaknesses and frailties had made me a less caring and compassionate person than I would like to have been. But, from that day on, and in spite of this self-awareness, I kept my distance from Shannon and oftentimes was not there for her when she needed me the most. I would always regret this.

When I got home that night, my husband expressed how proud he was of me. He told me that I had done the right thing by standing up for Ruben and coming forward with the truth. I wanted so badly to share with Ben my feelings and fears about Shannon's comments to the media, but I didn't. Ben was proud of me, and I was too afraid to reveal to him the real insensitive coward I had been toward Shannon. I was fearful of what he'd think of me. I couldn't sleep that night, and I drank a lot of milk to head off that inevitable upset stomach.

The day following the demonstration, Ruben and I had to face our other coworkers at the RAIC/Riverside. As always, Yolanda Rios was very supportive and even filled us in on the reactions around the office during the demonstration. Evantie, of course, had been embarrassed and was mad at us. As Yolanda told me this, I must admit, I was reveling in this first tiny taste of justice. Jerry Johnston smiled and gave me a big hug. He said, "You stinker! I can't believe you guys did this! What incredible courage you have." As did most everyone in the office, Jerry loved seeing Evantie squirm.

Most people didn't agree with our course of action, but everyone seemed pleased to see Evantie show some fear. I must admit, I got a total rush after hearing how this affected Evantie. I told Ruben, "Good! Let that s-o-b see how it feels to have the heat at his door." I was in this because I wanted to bring about some kind of justice, but what I came to realize was that I also wanted to hurt and humiliate Evantie and the others like him in management. I kept thinking of the IA agents reading me my rights like I was a criminal. I thought of how I was passed over for promotion by the agency that couldn't investigate their way out of a paper bag. I found that what I was craving was revenge, something to which I thought I was immune.

A couple of days after the demonstration, our new Group Supervisor, Lewis Cohen, called me into his office. Expecting some sort of retaliation, I thought to myself, "Oh no! Here it goes." Then as I was coming down the hall he told me to bring my tanker car case with me." I gathered up my stuff and met him in his office. He asked me for the whole history of the rail project and also wanted information on my criminal cases. I found him to be surprisingly supportive of me and my concerns. As the conversation developed, I felt more and more comfortable speaking somewhat candidly about Evantie and Brinkley's undermining of my case and of the rail project. I held back the information that Ervin Rios, Ruben, Renado and I had dug up which pointed a corruption finger square at Brinkley's crooked face. I still saw Lewis as management, and, therefore, not to be trusted.

After briefing Lewis, he told me that he felt I had done a good job on the project and the case so far. He shared with me that he, too, had gone up against Brinkley once, and had come out with the short end of the stick. He thought that the rail project was a viable one and that I should have been given more support. "Darlene," he said, "you're caught in the middle of a political machine. On one hand, no one else has the extensive knowledge, extensive training or the interest in this rail stuff, and on the other hand, you've made one hell of a seizure and gained important information into the Arellano-Felix Organization." He continued, "I want you to write a rail project, and I am going to try to ram-rod it through." "You mean rewrite it, don't you?" I replied. "I already had the project written and up and running when it was derailed by Brinkley, and we all know what that's all about, now don't we?" He laughed, "Derailed, ha, that's a funny pun. Darlene, having a spine is not always popular or politically correct for one's career. Believe me, I know."

I stared into his eyes with distrust and curiosity. What was his angle? Why was he acting like he was going to help me? Why would he go up against Brinkley after he had seen what had happened to us? Lewis was new, had only been at the office for a couple of weeks, and I had yet to size him up. He looked back into my eyes as if he sensed I was trying to read him. He paused, sighed and said, "Look, take what you've done, update it, and put it in the new project proposal format. Darlene, I'm not your enemy here. I believe in this project, and I'm going to help you get past the political stumbling blocks that are currently in your way." I asked him, "Even if that means going up against Brinkley?" He responded, "I did it once, and I'm not afraid to do it again." We both sat there staring at each other, trying to read each others' minds, looking for a flinch or some telltale sign to help figure each other out. Finally, I took a deep breath, got up and said, "OK, you got it. First draft will be on your desk by tomorrow morning." Lewis responded, "Hey, whoa! I don't expect you to have this done by tomorrow. Take a week at least." I responded in my determined "Captains" tone of voice, "You'll have it on your desk tomorrow, sir."

Lewis started laughing and in a sweet tone of voice said, "Darlene, sit back down here for a minute and talk to me, let's just talk, OK?" I paused for a minute and sat back down. "Look," he said, "I understand agents like you and Jerry. You're not like the rest of these guys. Your military background and brainwashing is a big part of you. I know; I was a Naval officer. I know how you guys think: duty and honor above all else. Hell, I admire that in you! But still, you've got to play politics sometimes … everyone does." There was a long pause and I just sat there looking at him with an expression of "Why the hell are you telling me this?" Then he completely changed the subject and asked, "So, how's the Olympics training going? I know you were working hard on cutting your time on your flip turns. Did you ever get Mike to work with you on that?" "Yeah," I said, "he showed me a better technique for coming off the wall that not only cut time, but relieved the pressure on my shoulder injury." We continued the small talk with him trying to win my trust through a display of interest and concern about my proceeding to train with injuries. Then he asked me if I could put together a meeting with the federal prosecutor and the powers that be, the Customs Inspectors and the locals involved in the rail project. I told him I thought that was a good idea, and I'd see to it.

The next day at 1100hrs, I placed the draft of the "new improved" rail project on Lewis' desk with a note telling him that the meeting would be at the U.S. Attorney's office on Monday morning at 0900hrs.

I had lunch with Ruben and Renado the next day at the usual dive and briefed them on the "warm and fuzzy" conversation I had with Lewis. They weren't sure what to think of it either, but Renado committed to be at the rail meeting. "Don't worry, guys," he said, "I'll get a fix on this and point this boy Lewis in the right direction."

On Monday morning, most of the parties involved in the rail project met. Lewis, Ervin, Renado, AUSA Yvette and Chief O'Leary were there.

We made small talk at first and then Yvette pointblank asked Lewis who was torpedoing the rail project. Lewis answered, in front of everyone, "Drake Brinkley." Then Yvette asked him why, but he didn't have an answer. Yvette looked at me with great concern and then back at Lewis with great suspicion. We did some brainstorming and Lewis handed out my second version of the new "Operation Lite Rail" proposal.

After the meeting, Renado, Ervin and I stayed behind to meet with Yvette. I updated Renado and Yvette on the suspicions and information Ervin and I had put together. Renado looked at Yvette and said, "Do you want to know what I think? I'll tell you what I think…Darlene stumbled into one serious case here." Renado looked at me and said, "You weren't supposed to find that loaded tanker car, and they certainly don't want you over there finding another one. And do you know what else? I think this Brinkley guy is crooked as hell, and all of you guys are in danger." Yvette's face showed great concern and even fear as she listened. I looked at Renado and said, "What do you mean, 'you guys?' You've been in the middle of this since day one, boy. If they miss me, the bullet will probably hit you."

Former Customs Inspector and well-publicized San Diego whistle-blower, John Carman, had previously told us of an FBI agent out of San Diego, who was already looking into the border corruption issues related to the Hydro tanker car seizure. He had suggested that we all go talk to him. I got his name and number and made an appointment to see him.

Ervin Rios, Sandy Nunn, Ruben Sandoval, Clark Janice, John Carman and I met with FBI Special Agent William Motts. We briefed him on everything that we had put together thus far, and he seemed totally overwhelmed. The whole time we were briefing him, he had a look of bewilderment and was clearly beginning to realize the scope of the work. I sensed that for FBI Agent Motts, it looked like too much work and a political nightmare.

Ten days after the demonstration, Ruben was called into Evantie's office with Lewis in tow, and Evantie read Brinkley's proposal to give Ruben 45 days on the bricks, administrative time off without pay. I was at the gym working out when I got the page. We met at the usual place with Renado. Ruben was both livid and worried, and rightfully so. He knew this would kill him financially, as he and his wife just had a new little baby boy. Renado and I tried to console him.

The next day, I walked into the office and passed by David Gray. I looked at him briefly and said, "Hey." He looked back at me with an evil expression. I knew that his IA thug buddies had already clued him in on the impending attempted rape investigation. I felt afraid and immediately regretted leaving my gun in the trunk of my G-ride. I sat at my desk working on reports and waited for the hammer to drop. Gray passed by my doorway, and then hit the wall in the hallway outside my office so hard that one of my pictures fell off. Ruben wasn't there, and I was becoming more scared and angry by the minute.

After a few minutes, Gray pounded on my wall again. I thought he was going to put his fist through it. My fear turned to rage, and I felt my blood boiling. I had a tennis racquet next to my desk, and I took it and walked down the hall towards Gray's office. I swung the racquet against the metal frame on his door. Gray was startled and jumped in his chair. I looked at him with a challenging glare and said in a low, deliberate tone of voice, "Oh, sorry, Gray. Am I disturbing you?" He looked at me a bit startled and looked back at his computer, ignoring me. I regained control of my temper and walked back to my office. My chest was pounding, and my face was hot.

A little while later, Ruben walked in. I told him what had just happened. He walked over to me, squatted down next to my chair and whispered to me very firmly, "Now, you better listen to me. You had better start carrying your p-shooter. I mean it. I don't want to see you unarmed anymore. That crazy bastard, Gray, is likely to do anything, and I don't want to see you get hurt. If I let you get hurt, Ben will kill me." I smiled at him and said meekly, "Oh, little man, don't worry. I have a tennis racquet." Ruben rose up and said, "Give me that," and grabbed the racquet away from me. I made a funny face at him, and he couldn't help laughing. He shook his head at me, holding back a grin, but I could see the concern on his face.

That night the dream returned. I was standing in the Daniel Boone National Forest on a trail overlooking the waterfalls at Cumberland Falls State Park. I immediately recognized the location. This was one of my most favorite places growing up. I used to sit for hours listening to the relaxing sound of the water as it flowed over the falls. I would watch the water go over the falls, mesmerized. Here I was again, feeling the cool rocks on the overhang above my head. The air was fresh, cool and crisp. Everything was so brilliantly colored with the colors of fall. It was beautiful, and I never wanted to leave there again. I looked down the familiar trail and saw the toddler standing there. He was still filthy and stared at me with his big, deep blue eyes and melted my heart. I walked toward him, and he smiled. I knew he was about to take me somewhere else and I spoke to him, "Please, let us stay here for just a little while." He smiled in an impish little way, and then I was somewhere else.

We were at the farm again. The toddler took me by the hand, and I picked him up. I walked to the top of the small hill and could see the farm at the other side of the hill. I immediately looked for the corral. There he was, the strange young man. He was sitting on the back of an old flatbed truck. The bed of the truck and the side railings were made of wooden planks. It reminded me of an old truck that my grandfather had. He used it to take feed to the cows and horses. I could only see the young man through the wooden planks. He was dressed the same, was smoking and dangling his legs back and forth. On the tailgate next to him, he had a styrofoam cup of tea. I could see the tag of the tea bag hanging out of the cup. I heard him talking in his strange accent. His voice was deep and soft. He was talking to the ducks and chickens. He had something he was feeding them. He seemed relaxed and at peace with himself, not at all how he was in my dream of him at the Shrine Auditorium. This is where he belonged. I took a deep breath and noticed how beautiful everything was. I noticed that I, too, was at peace with myself. I walked closer to the truck in an effort to see his face. Something stopped me, and I felt frustration. I could only see the side of his face through the wooden planks. But I saw his eyes again, eyes that captivated me, deep blue like the ocean. I wanted to yell to him to get his attention, but I couldn't. In a split second, I was awake.

I lay there pondering the dream. Why was I dreaming this? What did it mean? If this was the angel of death, why was he smoking and talking to poultry? If this was some type of message, why didn't anyone ever talk to me? Was I supposed to purchase stock in poultry and tea today? Why was the toddler always dirty and pitiful looking? Why couldn't I ever see the man's face? Why was it that every time I started feeling relaxed and at peace with myself, that little toddler jerked me somewhere else, or I awoke? I tried to put it all out of my mind. I was still afraid of telling anyone about these dreams for fear that this information might get into the wrong hands. The "enemy," the corrupt Customs managers and IA, would have a field day with something like this! They could say that I was "nuts" and use it to attack my credibility. I could just imagine Evantie laughing in my face as he took my badge and gun and put me on stress leave because of my dreams. I would never give him that satisfaction.

On May 25, 1999, I got a call from Sandy. She told me that the someone from management had just called her in and given her a letter of disciplinary action, which included three days on the bricks beginning today. She was so angry but had the intelligence to see that this was only proving our point and making our future litigation easier. I talked to her and her mom later that evening. I could tell that her mom was getting very worried. I felt sorry for Sandy's mom and was glad that I had decided not to tell my parents anything about what was going on. I had heard the concern in Sandy's mom's voice, and as a parent, I completely understood and empathized with her.

Chapter Twenty-three

Another Surprise

On May 26, 1999, Sandy and I had lunch with ex-Customs Special Agent Ron Bundy. Ron was one of the first people that I met when I swore-in with Customs. Ron had recently retired after suffering abuses similar to what we were suffering at the hands of Drake Brinkley. Ron was a money laundering and fraud expert who had worked large U.C. (undercover) projects with David Gray. Over lunch, Sandy and I filled him in on what had been happening to us and the role that David Gray had been playing. Ron responded, "None of this surprises me at all, Darlene. Don't you get it? David Gray is crazy about you and has been for years." "What!" I exclaimed. "Where are you getting this from? No way!" Ron said, "Don't you remember that Christmas Party several years ago at the U.C. off-site? Do you remember that someone stole one of your shoes, a red pump? It was Gray. For two weeks after that party, all any of us ever heard about from him was, "Oh, Darlene this, and oh, Darlene that; he couldn't stop talking about you, and how great you looked in your red dress and shoes. That nut carried your shoe around for days and kept it on his desk. We all thought he was loco."

I was in shock. I had no idea. I told him, "Ron, none of this makes sense. Gray's happily married." Ron said, "I'm telling you, Darlene, married or not, this guy is obsessed with you. Don't you remember how he was trying so hard to get you assigned to the U.C. project permanently? And if he hadn't gotten transferred to IA, with his pull, he would have gotten his way. Why, he even told everyone that's why he was putting in to return back to RAIC/Riverside...to work with you, the infamous

Darlene." I said, "Well, I *was* wondering why he made it a point to move into the same office as Ruben and I." Ron responded, "Exactly. He fully expected that you and he would partner up because of your previous friendship, and that he would worm his way into a relationship with you. Then when he was sent to do management's dirty work on Ruben, you did the unexpected. You stood up for Ruben against Gray." I said, "I stood up for the truth, and defended my partner against discrimination and retaliation." Ron said, "Yeah, but that's not how Gray sees it. He sees it like this: you and he go way back, before Ruben. He thought that since you were so close, you would naturally side with him against Ruben; and when you didn't, Gray saw it as betrayal."

Sandy said, "You know this all makes perfect sense; I knew that Gray always acted like a jilted lover around you." "Jilted lover!" I replied. "This is ridiculous! We were only friends. The man never even made a serious pass at me. He knew I loathed married men who cheat." Ron said, "Trust me, Darlene, Gray would have picked and chosen his timing carefully, then he would have found you at a vulnerable moment and wormed his way into your life. Dar, this guy sees Ruben as the guy that stole you away from him." I said, "This doesn't make any sense. Ruben and I are both happily married, and we've never even contemplated having any type of romantic relationship. This is crazy!" Ron said, "No, it's not, Dar. That's your perception. Gray doesn't know the relationship that you and Ruben have; he only thinks that you dumped him for Ruben." Sandy nodded her head in agreement. "Darlene, I've seen how David Gray looks at you. He's in love with you and blames Ruben for turning you against him." Ron agreed and said, "Exactly. Face it Darlene, Gray has it in for Ruben, and it's more than just doing the dirty work for management."

Of course, I went home in total shock. Had I been so naive that I hadn't seen this? Had I misjudged Gray's feelings about me all along? Could this be true? Poor Ruben! I felt so guilty. Ruben was apparently on the receiving end of Gray's revenge because of me. I told my husband what

Ron and Sandy had told me, and much to my surprise, Ben agreed. "That doesn't surprise me at all, honey. You remember, I was at several of these parties, and I, too, saw how Gray acted around you. They're right. It's obvious." "How the hell did I miss this one?" I asked. "I'm supposed to be a trained investigator. What's wrong with me?"

"Darlene, when it comes to these things, you are a bit naive. You don't realize how you look and the effect that you have on men. I mean, you reeled me in, didn't you?" Then Ben tickled me and got me to laugh with him. "Don't worry, Dar, Ruben's a big boy. He doesn't hold you responsible for Gray's behavior. Ruben's smarter than that. You and Ruben just keep sticking together, no matter what."

Chapter Twenty-four

The Ultimate Price

On May 28, 1999, I got a 911 page from Sandy. I called her back, and she was hysterical. She told me that her dad had just died of a heart attack. She was crushed. Sandy and her dad, Rocky, were very close. Rocky Nunn was a veteran Air Force pilot, and a 20 year veteran of the Immigrations Service. He was a well-known, well-respected and loved man, married to his wife, Jean, for nearly 50 years.

Ruben, Ervin, Shannon and I all attended the funeral. Rocky was buried with full military honors and a formal salute from the Border Patrol. Sandy's poor mom looked shattered and frail, and Sandy's face displayed the look of an anguished, broken heart. My heart ached for them both. After the funeral, we went to lunch and Sandy told me that her mom had said that Rocky had been so worried about what was going on with the retaliation Sandy was experiencing. One of the things he had told his wife was that he felt helpless. "I'm old and weak," he said, "and I can't help my daughter." Jean relayed Rocky's despair when he heard of the suspension Sandy received as a result of the Customs IA investigation. I went home that night, called my dad, laughed with him and told him I loved him. Of all the things that had happened to any of us, Rocky's death was the straw that broke the camel's back. This wonderful man lost his life worrying about his daughter suffering at the hands of men like Drake Brinkley. This price was too high to pay. Sandy later went back to her father's grave and vowed to Rocky that she would not stop fighting the system until justice was done.

I had been training hard for the Police Olympics, and all too quickly, it was here. It was the second and third week of June 1999, and I had entered three events: a cross-country 10k run and two swimming events. The 10k took place on equestrian trails at a park in Pasadena, California. When the race began, I knew we had problems when the sign read "Advanced Riders Only." It was one of the toughest cross-country courses I had ever run. It reminded me of being back in the military. It was challenging and fun, and I managed to survive.

The swimming events took place at the Aquatic Center in Pasadena, California. My first event was at 0900 in the morning. I had to commute two hours to the center and needed to arrive an hour before check-in. I hardly slept the night before, nervous and anxious about the events. It was cold that morning, and I couldn't seem to get warmed up. I completed my first event and laid down on one of the benches. As the sun came out, warming my tired body, I fell fast asleep. I awoke suddenly to hear them calling my next event. The other swimmers were already behind the blocks. I ran over to the event sign-in table, forgetting my event card. I was still half asleep and ran back to get my card. When I got to my block, the other swimmers were already there looking at me in disapproval for making them wait. Over the loud speaker I heard, "Swimmers take your mark." I jumped up on to the block and got into position. Then I heard, "Stand down, stand down. Lane seven, would you remove your sunglasses, please." I then noticed that all the other swimmers were laughing at me, and I realized they were talking about me. I stepped down, removed my glasses and put my goggles on. I felt like such a bonehead. Clearly, I was suffering from the nonstop stress.

I ended up taking two silver medals in the Police Olympics. The following Monday, Brinkley put out a SAIC/LA office wide email message congratulating everyone who took medals at the Police Olympics. Everyone's name was listed but mine. How childish this was! But, I told myself it didn't matter. I didn't compete for U.S. Customs anyway. I just wanted to set a good example for my kids and make them proud. But it still hurt. When Ruben got into the office, I showed him my medals. He gave me a big hug and told me how proud he was. Then Jerry Johnston walked in, saw the medals and gave me a high-five. I told them about how I had made a fool of myself by forgetting to remove my sunglasses on the block, and they both cracked up. I showed Ruben the email from the SAIC office. He couldn't believe it. "Man," he said, "that's low. What a bunch of idiots!" I told him it was no big deal, and I tried to conceal my hurt, but I knew he could tell.

Later that morning we had an office meeting. Jerry congratulated me in front of everyone. Ruben was not pleased and I could tell he was about to say something, so I kicked him in the shins under the table, and subtly shook my head "no." Lewis acted impressed and sincerely congratulated me, as did several others. Evantie just sat there, glared at me with a condescending smirk, and refused to recognize my accomplishments in any way. I caught myself staring at him as I was thinking some wicked things about him, and I noticed he was looking back wondering what I was about to say or do. I took a deep breath, got up and walked out of the meeting. My angry thoughts scared me, and I knew this email-snub was designed to bait me. I was known as the "Hothead," and I knew that I had better not react. I knew that if I ever really lost it, I would give them just the type of ammunition they were looking for to fire me, or worse.

On July 18, 1999, I received a response from Customs Regional EEO Complaint Center on one of the EEO complaints of retaliation I had previously filed. Contained therein, was a statement from EEO Supervisor Ms. Mary Conales, stating that it was in fact she who in 1997, turned my EEO file (containing Sandy's statement) over to IA. It was two full years later, and she was finally admitting this. For two years, Conales had conveniently omitted the fact that she did this. She had made two sworn statements dissuading that what we were receiving could have been retaliation, since there was no way that, at the time, management could have known about our complaints. I showed this to

Ruben and he immediately recognized the significance of this. At the time that Conales turned my packet over to IA, Elaine Black was the head of IA, and her second in command was Stella O'Shea, wife of Dudley O'Shea. Dudley and Drake Brinkley were tight friends, and Elaine Black became, and was currently the ASAIC under Brinkley. Additionally, this leak happened while David Gray was working in IA. Therein lies the much-needed nexus of how management knew full well who was filing complaints, and thus the retaliation. When I faxed this to our attorney, Tom, he said that it was golden! Conales was toast, or so I thought.

On July 20, 1999, Ruben and I were in the office completing reports. Lewis came to the doorway and said, "Ruben, Evantie and I need to see you in Evantie's office." Ruben and I looked at each other with dread, both knowing that this was going to be Ruben's sentencing for his 45-day suspension without pay. Ruben looked at Lewis and said, "I'm not going in there without a witness," and as he stood up he said, "Let's go, Dar." We all walked into Evantie's office as Evantie sat there looking at a document with a smug look. I wanted so badly to kick that chair out from under him to wipe that smirk off his face. I thought it would be more than justice for Evantie's ego to be knocked on his rear end by a girl. I caught myself dreaming about slapping him around in front of everybody.

Evantie told us to sit down. Ruben and Lewis sat down, and I took up a firm, almost military at-ease standing position against the door. This was a small act of defiance on my part. Evantie began reading Ruben's letter of suspension. With each condescending word, I could see Ruben's knuckles turning white as he squeezed the arms on his chair. I was somewhat surprised at Lewis' reaction. He was visibly disgusted with this and was throwing Evantie some pretty disrespectful looks. Had I underestimated him? Evantie then asked for Ruben's badge, weapon and keys. The look on Ruben's face was a combination of disbelief and helplessness. All I felt was rage. Ruben turned over his badge and gun and said, "My keys are at my desk." Evantie looked at me and said, "Can you go get them for us, Dar?" I stood there glaring at Evantie. I was truly looking into the face of the most uncompassionate, evil person I had ever met. He was clearly enjoying the moment.

Evantie said condescendingly, "Uh, Dar, the keys." I took a deep breath, and Lewis, anticipating that I was about to do something stupid, stood up and gently placed his hand on my arm. Lewis was talking to Ruben and looking into my eyes at the same time. "Ruben, I'll show you how to file an appeal on this in my office," Lewis said as he squeezed my arm as if to subtly say, don't do this, come with me, we'll handle this. I looked Lewis in the eyes, took a deep breath and subtly nodded my head up and down. Ruben got up, looked at Lewis and said, "You know this is bull–, don't you?" Lewis looked at Evantie with a look of agreement and said, "Come on guys, let's go to my office and talk." Evantie looked at Lewis with disgust, having been betrayed by a "fellow" manager.

I stopped in the office foyer by the sign-in/sign-out board and looked at Ruben. I could see the anger and worry on his face, and I felt so helpless, knowing that there was nothing I could do to help him. I was afraid I might start crying and refused to let anyone, especially Evantie, see this. "Where you going?" Lewis said. I responded, "I'll catch you later; Ruben, I'll be back in a bit and drive you home." I signed out and drove over to the UP rail yard, in Colton.

I sat on the hill overlooking the rail yard, watching the tanker cars moving onto the hump to be weighed. My mind was racing. I was sure that this railcar stuff was mostly what all this was about. Renado had been right from the beginning, and Ruben and I didn't see it soon enough. I felt so bad for Ruben. I knew how badly this would hit him financially. I kept replaying Evantie's arrogance in my mind but it did nothing but increase my anger. I drove to a Jack 'N The Box for a milkshake. As I drove through the drive-thru window, I remembered how it was Ruben who taught me that in Spanish "Jack-In-The-Box" was "Joaquin en la caja." I didn't want to go back to the office, but I wanted to be the one to drive Ruben home. I knew that's what he would want, and he deserved this loyalty.

As I pulled back into the parking garage of our office, I saw Evantie. Hitler himself, walking toward his G-ride. A very dark thought came over me. I imagined myself gunning my engine and running him over. I saw the act of running him over as stomping out pure evil incarnate. Just then I was startled by someone beeping their horn behind me. I took a deep breath, shook my head, looked back towards Evantie and saw that he had made it to his car. I could not believe how he and other corrupt U.S. Customs managers had turned me into somebody I did not want to be. I had become revengeful, bordering on irrational, and I didn't like what I had become.

On the way to Ruben's house, neither of us spoke much. I tried to reassure him that everything was going to work out, and that he had a lot of people who cared for him and would show their loyalty. I fumbled around trying to show some compassion and did a miserable job of it. I was never any good at showing the compassion that was truly in my heart. Any attempt at being soft or compassionate with adults, would cause this strange, embarrassing feeling to come over me. The only time that I didn't feel like this, the only time I felt comfortable showing compassion or being soft, was with my kids.

The 45 days that Ruben was gone were tough. Meanwhile, either Lewis and/or AUSA Yvette put pressure on someone in management, because suddenly I was back on the rail project. On August 2, 1999 I had put in for the Customs Physical Fitness Specialist School, at the Cooper Clinic in Dallas, Texas. Two days later, I got my memo back with Evantie's handwriting on it stating that Brinkley was not sending anyone. When I submitted my request, I also sent my memo to the Regional Fitness Director, Peter Blake. Blake had called me back upon receiving my memo and told me that there were several funded positions, and he had submitted my application to headquarters. What a contradiction.

Several days later, my school selection packet came from headquarters. I showed Lewis the memo from Evantie, the memo from Blake and the packet I'd received from headquarters. I knew this was putting Lewis in a tight spot, but I needed to know if I could trust him or not, and this would be a good test. I told Lewis that several years before, his predecessor, Ivan Winkowsky, had chiseled me out of attending this school. I told him how schools were scarce then, and I had to compete for the school based on my background and experience. I was selected 'most qualified' not only at the RAIC level, but also for the entire SAIC office.

Lewis seemed sincere when he said, "Dar, I'm going to take care of this. This time you will be going." A couple of hours later, Lewis poked his head in my door and said, "Pack your bags; you're going to Dallas." Later that day, Yolanda Rios, our office Investigative Assistant, told me that she had heard Lewis in Evantie's office, and they were arguing about something regarding me. I felt a new sense of trust in Lewis, and it felt good. At this point, there were only a select few people I felt I could trust. The RAIC/Riverside was a pretty grim place to work. I knew that Evantie would see Lewis' defense of me as betrayal. Evantie, of course, would blame me for the betrayal and would view it as an "end-run" around him. I knew Evantie would have to 'get even,' and again try to put me in my place.

The day before I left for Dallas, we had an office meeting. Lewis mentioned that I was going to be gone for a week at the fitness school, and Evantie arrogantly responded, "Well, I hope you don't come back here thinking that you're gonna try to whip us into shape or anything." I looked at him and noticed his pack of cigarettes lying on the table in front of him (Evantie was a chain smoker). I pushed the cigarettes toward him and said, "No, Lawrence, I'm gonna come back here and buy you a carton of cigarettes." Everyone laughed, and Evantie fumed because I'd embarrassed him. Even though I knew that he'd make me pay, I just couldn't help myself. Then Evantie made a rather interesting announcement. He stated that Brinkley had recently reiterated an earlier policy regarding the use of vehicles and was intent on enforcing it. "You all know how 'hands-on' Brinkley is when it comes to vehicles," he said. I kicked Ruben under the table, and we smiled at each other. This was in direct contradiction to what Brinkley had testified to, under oath, in the deposition for Ruben's civil case. Brinkley stated that he had nothing to do with vehicles and that anything related to vehicles was assigned to someone else. We knew all along that Brinkley had lied about his responsibilities under oath, and now we had a room full of witnesses!

Chapter Twenty-five

Twisting the Knife

I left the next day for a wonderful, peaceful week in Dallas. I was able to put Customs out of my mind, if only just for a while. The Monday I returned, I signed-on to check my email. There was a message from headquarters congratulating the top three "SPS" (Significant Problem Solving) Projects. Operation Lite Rail (my rail project) won an award for one of the best projects of the year. Then they listed the names of all the Customs employees who had participated. Each participant was to receive a Commissioner's Citation and $1000. Everyone on the project was listed but me, and there was no reference to all the work AUSA Yvette had done either. I was in shock. My heart just sank. This wasn't just a knife in the back, this was twisting the already existing knife for a final death blow to my spirit.

I printed out the message, grabbed it and stormed into Evantie's office. I thought I might like to cram the message down the s-o-b's throat. I slammed my fist on Evantie's door. I suddenly noticed Yolanda and Lewis standing next to me. "He's gone; he's gone," Yolanda said. Lewis asked me what was wrong, and I gave the memo to him, turned to Yolanda and asked her where he was. Yolanda was taken aback and didn't answer. I ran to her desk and flipped through Evantie's appointment book. He had gone on leave for a week. I went to my office, grabbed my keys and started for the door, determined to take some time off. Lewis tried to talk to me as I was signing out. He said, "Dar, I hope you know that I had nothing to do with this." I ignored him and walked out.

I went home, called my husband and began crying. I wasn't making sense to him, and he was worried. All of the anger, frustration and helplessness of two years of emotional abuse finally caught up with me. I had watched people I cared about be harassed, humiliated and beaten down. I called in sick the next day and began looking for another job.

On September 1, 1999, Sandy Nunn resigned in disgust from the U.S. Customs Service. The day that she resigned, we celebrated. She seemed totally free, felt great about her decision, and I envied her. She had secured a good position in private industry, and this inspired me to do the same. At her going away luncheon, I presented her with a plaque from the ACEC that stated, "for demonstrating courage against insurmountable odds." How appropriate those words were. I was proud of her.

On September 15, 1999, I completed my second interview with a solid company in private industry and was selected. On September 16, I submitted my letter of resignation with two weeks notice to my supervisor, Lewis. Remarkably, he seemed in total shock and disbelief. He tried vigorously to talk me out of it, but it was to no avail. When I walked back to my office, Ruben was waiting for me. He already knew what I had decided to do. He and I had spoken several times about the company I was interviewing with, and he was happy for me. I sat down and let him read my resignation letter.

As he was reading, Jerry Johnston walked in. "What's going on, folks?" Ruben handed him the letter. He actually dropped down into a chair and began to tear up. He, too, tried to talk me out of it but eventually gave up and gave me a big hug, and said, "I'm gonna miss you. Who's gonna give me crap and keep me straight around here?" I felt like a captain abandoning the loyal crew. In some ways, I felt like I had failed and was running away from a fight, but I knew the time had finally arrived. I began boxing things up from my desk and taking down my photos from my wall. One was the photo from the tanker car case where I was on top of the car waving at everyone. I walked it over to Ruben and hung it on his bulletin board. "Hey, pizanno, if you miss me, just look at me waving at you here in this picture." Ruben was teary eyed, too, and gave me a big hug. "God, how I wish I was going with you Dar, you lucky thing, you." It was amazing how the corruption and abuse of the U.S. Customs management had scarred us so. But I was lucky—I could leave.

Chapter Twenty-six

Letting Go and Moving On

On September 24, 1999, I walked into Evantie's office for the last time. Lewis was with me as I turned in my badge, weapon and bulletproof vest. As I laid my badge on the table, I didn't feel the joy that Sandy displayed; I didn't feel sadness. I felt nothing. The badge that for so many years meant justice and honor to me, now lay on Evantie's table as a badge of dishonor, tarnished by managers like Drake Brinkley, Lawrence Evantie and Harrison Wells. Lewis tried one more time to talk me out of resigning, but I politely ignored him.

Ruben and Jerry walked me down to Ruben's car to take me home. We stopped at the rear of the car, and Jerry put his hands in his pockets, looked at me in disbelief and said, "So that's it, huh?" I looked at him, smiling and said, "That's it." Jerry hung his head, looked at the ground and struggled for words. "Darlene, don't do this. Let's just walk back upstairs, get your stuff back and go catch bad guys." I looked into his eyes and they began tearing up. I put my hand out to shake his and he grabbed my hand and pulled me into a long hug. I was leaving so many good, close friends. "I'm gonna miss you, my Kentucky gal." As Ruben drove me away, I looked back at Jerry standing there in the garage watching us go. He stood there watching, looking so pitiful. I felt like I'd let him and my other buddies down.

Ruben and I talked only about my new job and how lucky I was to start my new life away from Customs. He said he was happy for me and that made the trip home easy for both of us. He helped me unload all the stuff I had brought home from the office, and I could sense his

extreme discomfort. Ruben, much like me, had a real problem express-
ing any emotion other than anger. He had been my trusted partner for
seven years, through thick and thin, good and bad, and now it was end-
ing because of unbelievable incompetence and management abuses—it
wasn't fair!

He gave me a quick hug, told me he would call me soon and jumped
into his car and sped off. I knew he was hurting and thought I had left
him behind and alone against Evantie and Brinkley. I hoped he would
come to understand that this was something that I just had to do, not
just for me, but also for my family. My family needed a whole person,
not some physically shattered woman in a daily rage. My husband and
kids deserved better, and I was going to give it to them.

I often thought about what I'd miss most about the job, and I knew it
would be the people. I missed my old mentor and surrogate father, Bob
Mattivi, who always took time from his busy schedule to guide me in
the right direction with his good judgment. He lightened up the mood
with his wit. I missed Jerry Johnston, my fellow kindred spirit from
Kentucky. Jerry was always so gentle and soft-spoken and added calm-
ness to any situation. He had something a 'type-A' personality like me
needed. He seemed to understand me more than anyone else in the
office. Our backgrounds were so similar. I missed Yolanda, the
Investigative Aid. She was like a surrogate big sister to me, always watch-
ing my back. She truly was a super lady. I had more laughs with her and
Bob in a short time than I probably would have for the rest of my life. I
missed my partner Ruben, my best friend, only second to my husband,
Ben. He was like a big brother to me and made the job seem easier. I
missed Renado and all of his jokes and kidding around, but most of all
I missed the noble loyalty. It was like we were all family, and I was being
forced to move away from my home by an evil corruption that we could
not control.

That night I dreamed again. I was in my old Customs office, the orig-
inal office when I came to work in Riverside, talking to Jerry, Ruben and

Mattivi. We were joking and laughing, and I felt warm and loved. I looked down the hallway, and there stood the toddler. I didn't recognize him at first. This time he was clean and beautiful. He was healthy, happy and smiling. I walked over to him and picked him up. He smelled wonderful. He had that distinct "baby smell," like my kids used to have as babies. I took a deep breath of him and closed my eyes. When I opened my eyes we were back on the farm. Everything was beautiful and brightly colored. The green grass waved in the wind, and I could feel the cool spring-like breeze on my face. I put the toddler down, and we walked to the top of the small hill. There the farm lay in the beautiful little valley with cows grazing on the nearby pastures. I heard the young man's deep, soft voice say, "Hello mates" in his British/Australian accent.

I looked to the left and next to the old pickup truck was the handsome young man I'd seen so many times before, but this time his back was not facing me. He was slowly walking towards us with a cute, knowing smile. His eyes were a beautiful blue and gleamed like the ocean. The toddler took my hand, looked up at me smiling as if to say, "Go on, its OK." I walked towards the young man, and as I got closer I felt more and more at peace with myself. I was light and free! I felt as though I had known him all my life, like a long lost friend I was so happy to find again. It was strange though, I had no romantic or passionate feelings towards him. This was not a romantic or sexual thing. It was as if I were looking into the face of a beautiful male angel who came to lift me up and put peace back into my heart.

The young man gently took my hand, looked into my eyes very shyly, and smiled. He led me to the back of the pickup truck, picked me up and sat me down on the bed of the truck. He jumped up and sat down next to me. He had on a flannel shirt with a green T-shirt underneath and wore cowboy boots. The truck began to move while our feet dangled over the edge. As the truck rolled gently down the hill towards the pond, my tummy tickled from the movement, and we both laughed. I had no idea who was driving the truck and didn't care. I felt implicit trust in the young man, trust that I had all but lost in humans in the real world.

The truck stopped at the pond and backed up with the rear of the truck facing the water. The young man looked at the pond and the ducks, turned to me and asked, "Isn't this beautiful?" I nodded and smiled. The ducks swam over to us, and he gave me some breadcrumbs to feed them. We sat there in total peace and tranquility for what seemed like hours. The sun was warm, and I could hear birds singing. He looked at me and smiled and said, "Everything's going to be OK, you know?" I smiled back and studied his face.

I wanted to remember what he looked like when I awoke so that in the event I ever saw him again, I could recognize him. His face was handsome, but had a ruggedness about it. He seemed at peace with himself in this place, and he was somehow sharing this with me. I was grateful. I gently placed my hand on top of his and said, "Thank you." He looked at me and smiled and said, "You're going to be alright, mate. Everything's going to be alright."

The next morning my youngest son woke me up. He was standing there with his "holdey blanky" (his security blanket), smiling, and he said in his sweet little voice, "Momma, you're home!" And with that, I was home.

Epilogue

Former Special Agent Darlene Catalan moved her family to a small town back east. There, she and her family live a more tranquil life together, working to put the ugly events revealed in this book behind them.

Special Agent Ruben Sandoval still works for the Customs agency. Shortly after Darlene left, Ruben was again brought up on more bogus charges and IA investigations, as was the Office Investigative Aid, Yolanda Rios. Ironically, these phony charges were alleged only days after Ruben and Yolanda took part in the reporting of David Gray and Sherry King for the riding while drunk in Gray's G-ride incident. Ruben had taken over the rail project from Darlene, and he and Renado Gianini tried to cover each other's back, to no avail. The Tanker Car Case and the rail project were again ordered "closed" by Customs management. When Ruben reported this retaliation to all appropriate agencies, Ruben and Yolanda were subsequently suspended from access to the Department of Treasury's computer systems.

Former Special Agent Sandy Nunn is still leading the fight against discrimination, cronyism, and corruption within the Department of Treasury. Customs blackballed her in the law enforcement community, and she had a very hard time getting another job. Sandy, being the resilient fighter that she is, started her own business. As tough as all of this has been on her, she is still fighting back with the courage of a tiger in order to keep her promise to her dad. Sandy is in the process of writing a book of her own regarding many of these same issues. Look for "The Dark Side of Justice" due out in the near future.

As this book went to press, Ricardo Sandoval is still the RAIC/Calexico. Shortly after Customs lost an appeal in Ricardo's lawsuit, the Customs Office of Internal Affairs placed Ricardo under yet another bogus investigation.

Renado Gianini is still a supervisor for the San Bernardino Police Department, Intelligence Unit. He works closely with Ruben and tries to cover his back.

Ervin Rios is going back to college, taking evening and weekend classes. He vows to get his law degree someday, retire from Customs and protect whistleblowers against corrupt government managers.

AUSA Yvette Palazuelos has been appointed a judge in Los Angeles.

Senior Inspector Cathy Harris, after much pressure and force, has been rehired by Customs, and is actively involved with the CEADA (Customs Employees Against Discrimination Association) organization in their fight for justice. Cathy Harris has successfully authored and published a thrilling and accurate book about her ordeal entitled "Flying While Black: A Whistleblower's Story."

Shortly after Darlene resigned, former Inspector and fellow whistle-blower John Carmon of San Diego, California, was arrested on phony charges by the San Diego Police Department. This happened after the meeting with FBI Agent William Motts and the demonstration at RAIC/Riverside. Although Carmon was arrested by the San Diego Police Department, the arrest was based upon the influence and coercion of U.S. Customs Internal Affairs. The frame-up was clearly another retaliatory attack by Customs managers against a former employee for whistleblowing activities. All charges have been dismissed against him, and he is pursuing additional legal action against Customs.

SAIC/LA Drake Brinkley was allowed to retire with full benefits. This was in spite of the fact that numerous violations were reported against him, including evidence of corruption. Brinkley was recently appointed as a State Gaming Commissioner for a western state. Brinkley had bragged about his political connections, so the appointment was no surprise to those who knew him in cases unrelated to mine.

The Director of Customs Office of Internal Affairs, Harrison Wells, was fired, and a Grand Jury recently indicted him on allegations of perjury and corruption.

Mary Conales is still the Regional EEO Manager for Southern California in spite of all the numerous well-documented complaints and accusations filed against her.

There has been no known disciplinary action taken against David Gray for the many violations of policy and the attempted rape reported against him.

All allegations in this book have been reported to the FBI, the Office of Special Counsel, The Treasury Office of Inspector General, and to numerous members of the House and Senate. To date, there has been no congressional inquiry into these matters. In December 1999, Former Special Agents Catalan and Sandy Nunn, Senior Inspector Cathy Harris, along with other Federal Agent whistleblowers, were asked to speak at a Town Hall Meeting in Atlanta, GA. SA Catalan was quoted as saying, "Working for the U.S. Customs Service was like working for the Mafia."

Recommended Works

McAlary, Mike. *Good Cop Bad Cop* This story is about corruption and retaliation against whistleblowers in the NYPD. The commissioner of the NYPD at the time was Raymond Kelley. Kelley subsequently became the Commissioner of Customs and was commissioner during the timeframe that *U.S. Customs: Badge of Dishonor* and *Flying While Black* were written.

Flying While Black: A Whistleblower's Story by Cathy Harris.
Website: http://cathyharris.homestead.com

Former Customs Inspector and Whistleblower John Carmon has an excellent web site, a must see for anyone concerned about corruption and the war on drugs: http://www.customscorruption.com

Frontline: Drug Wars Interview with John E. Hensley.
Website: http://www.pbs.org/wgbh/pages/frontline/shows/drugs/interviews.html

Frontline: Drug Wars: Thirty Years of America's Drug War, a Chronology
Website: http://www.pbs.org/wgbh/pages/frontline/shows/drugs/cron/index.html

News Briefs: Law Enforcement section dated January-February 1999, entitled "U.S. Customs Service Admits Drug Corruption; Immigration Inspectors Indicted for Drug Corruption"
Website: http://www.ndsn.org/JANFEB99/LAWENF.html

NewsMax.com: article dated January 20, 2000 "Ex-Customs Agent
    Exposes Clinton 'Drug War'" by Carl Limbacher Jr.
    Website: http://www.newsmax.com/articles/?a=2000/1/20/35428

NewsMax.com–article dated April 20, 1997 "Inspector Alleges
    Corruption in Customs" by Christopher Ruddy
    Website: http://www.newsmax.com/
        articles/?a=1997/04/20/151505

DEA–Publications–Congressional Testimony–6/24/98; U.S. Department
    of Justice, Drug Enforcement Administration–Statement by:
    Donnie Marshall, DEA
    Website: http://www.usdoj.gov/dea/pubs/cngrtest/ct980624.htm

Darlene in Customs office at UPS sight, Ontario Airport

Darlene undercover as DHL delivery person

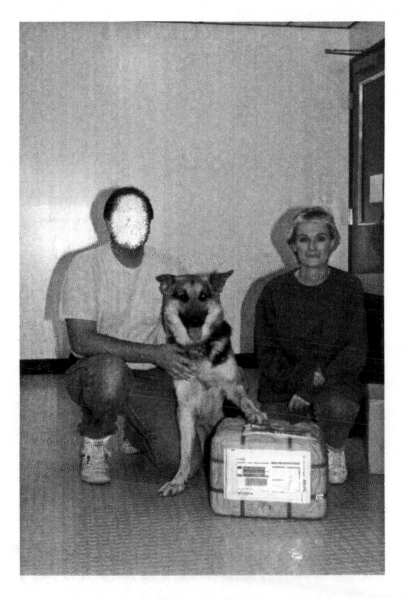

Darlene and seizure of 18lbs of raw opium

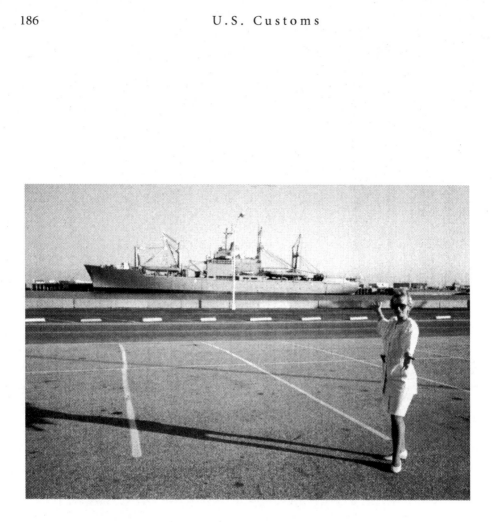

Darlene at Long Beach Naval Station

Darlene conducting inspection of suspected alien smugglers